LIFE IN YEAR ONE

ALSO BY SCOTT KORB

The Faith Between Us: A Jew and a Catholic
Search for the Meaning of God
(Coauthor Peter Bebergal)

The Harriet Jacobs Family Papers
(Associate Editor)

LIFE IN YEAR ONE

What the World Was Like
in First-Century Palestine

Scott Korb

RIVERHEAD BOOKS

a member of Penguin Group (USA) Inc.

New York

2010

RIVERHEAD BOOKS
Published by the Penguin Group
Penguin Group (USA) Inc., 375 Hudson Street, New York,
New York 10014, USA • Penguin Group (Canada), 90 Eglinton Avenue East,
Suite 700, Toronto, Ontario M4P 2Y3, Canada (a division of Pearson Penguin Canada
Inc.) • Penguin Books Ltd, 80 Strand, London WC2R 0RL, England • Penguin Ireland,
25 St Stephen's Green, Dublin 2, Ireland (a division of Penguin Books Ltd) • Penguin
Group (Australia), 250 Camberwell Road, Camberwell, Victoria 3124, Australia (a division
of Pearson Australia Group Pty Ltd) • Penguin Books India Pvt Ltd, 11 Community Centre,
Panchsheel Park, New Delhi–110 017, India • Penguin Group (NZ), 67 Apollo Drive, Rosedale,
North Shore 0632, New Zealand (a division of Pearson New Zealand Ltd) • Penguin Books
(South Africa) (Pty) Ltd, 24 Sturdee Avenue, Rosebank, Johannesburg 2196, South Africa

Penguin Books Ltd, Registered Offices: 80 Strand, London WC2R 0RL, England

Library of Congress Cataloging-in-Publication Data

Korb, Scott.
Life in year one : what the world was like in first-century Palestine / Scott Korb.
p.   cm.
Includes bibliographical references and index.
ISBN 978-1-59448-899-3
1. Palestine—History—To 70 A.D.   2. Palestine—Social life and customs—To 70 A.D.   I. Title.
DS112.K645   2010   2010000146
933'.05—dc22

Printed in the United States of America
1   3   5   7   9   10   8   6   4   2

BOOK DESIGN BY SUSAN WALSH

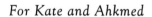

For Kate and Ahkmed

CONTENTS

Now every one needs food, clothing, and shelter. The lives of most men on earth are spent in getting these things. In our travels we shall wish to learn what our world brothers and world sisters eat, and where their food comes from. We shall wish to see the houses they dwell in and how they are built. We shall wish also to know what clothing they use to protect themselves from the heat and the cold.

—FRANK G. CARPENTER,
Around the World with the Children (1917)

—JAMES AGEE AND WALKER EVANS,
Let Us Now Praise Famous Men (1941)[1]

---

1. Agee seems to have made a few minor errors when quoting this geography primer at the beginning of *Let Us Now Praise Famous Men*. He also gets the author's name a little wrong. The epigraph above recovers the original wording from the 1917 book and restores Frank Carpenter's middle initial from B. to G. (i.e., George).

LIFE IN YEAR ONE

ON THE EPIGRAPHS
FOR *LIFE IN YEAR ONE*

Translating is making choices: a stream of decisions designed to capture something in the original language and deliver it to a new audience. It is impossible, whether we admit it or not, to translate without trying to *do something* with the material. We are, after all, human. Maybe we're trying to convey the beauty of a foreign poet, or maybe we're just trying to convince a pretty Parisian waitress to sit down and have a drink with us. Either way, translators always have goals, and these goals affect every decision we make. As readers of a translation, your first questions should always be "What is this person trying to accomplish?" and "How is he trying to accomplish it?"

To demonstrate what I mean, a favorite straw man in biblical translation, the beautiful King James Version, will be helpful. In 1604, King James I commissioned a new English-language Bible for the Church of England, translated from Hebrew, Greek, and a touch of Latin by forty-six clergymen and one eminent Greek scholar. It rapidly became the dominant translation. Here is its rendering of Matthew 5:6:

> Blessed are they which do hunger and thirst after
> righteousness: for they shall be filled.

This line is lousy with poetry. It conveys authority and inspires awe. How? Well, it starts with an inversion, "Blessed are they," instead of "They are blessed." This word order is archaic and literary, even in 1604. In other words, this isn't the way an average Londoner talked. Next we get the delicate phrasing of "they which" and the elaborated verb form "do hunger." Why these choices? For one, they fit the meter—oh yes, the first clause is written in an ancient poetic meter called dactylic pentameter. If that isn't fancy enough, we get "after" instead of a more common "for," a choice that suggests striving and effort (plus it too fits the meter).

So what is all this high-flown language meant to accomplish? Simple: To make you believe. To make a Christian out of those who aren't, and better Christians out of those who are. The translators created a Bible so sublimely beautiful, so removed from the world, that it could be easily accepted as the Word of God. They set out to *do something*, and they did it smashingly.

For the epigraphs to the chapters of *Life in Year One*, I've translated some very familiar Greek passages from the New Testament. All except the one heading the Epilogue came from the mouth of Jesus. Here, for example, is my version of that famous line from Matthew:

> Those who hunger and thirst for justice
> are blessed, since they will feast.

It has none of the heightened poetry: no meter, no delicate phrasing, no inversion. So what am I trying to do? Again the answer is simple—to put you there, on the street, at the time the words were spoken. As much as possible (and that is a *huge* qualifier), I have tried to recreate each line in its context. To do this, I've used a kind of informed imagining, gathering together everything I can know about the language, the historical setting, and the immediate circumstances, and then wading into that stream of choices.

So for this line, imagine with me: Jesus is on a hill, speaking to a crowd made up of people from all over Judea, Galilee, Jerusalem, and across the Jordan River. He isn't speaking in his first language, Aramaic. He talks in *koinē* Greek, a lingua franca, in order to be understood by Jews and Gentiles alike. His is a spoken language, a trade language, somewhat akin to Swahili in eastern Africa now; but still, *koinē* is degenerated from Classical and Hellenistic Greek, and has tremendous flexibility and force. With its philosophical and literary ancestry, it is a language with a diverse vocabulary, and yet the syntax has been ground down to bare essentials over centuries of use across the Mediterranean in marketplaces, courts, and army camps by non-native speakers. This is the language of the Gospels, full of simple phrases with blunt edges. Consider the class and (minimal) education of Jesus, his followers, and their audience, then ask, *What is Jesus trying to accomplish in these difficult circumstances—to be poetic, or to be understood?*

PATRICK STAYER

ON WRITING
LIFE IN YEAR ONE

Beware of those scholars aching to strut around in gaudy
robes, who love formal greetings in the markets, prime
seats in Synagogues, and places of honor at meals.

—LUKE 20:46

Listen to me—all of you—and pay attention.

—MARK 7:14

What goes into the mouth does not corrupt a man, but
what comes from the mouth, this corrupts a man.

—MATTHEW 15:11

The three quotations above—all fairly familiar, I think, and all from Jesus—are ones I tried to keep in mind as I wrote this book. The first, about strutting scholars, has been a reminder not to be arrogant, advice I find pretty useful whether I'm writing a book or not. Beyond that, the warning to be on guard against a certain kind of scholar has helped keep me mindful of the great many other dedicated and generous ones I've relied on in these pages: those women and men who have spent lifetimes poring over dusty religious and academic texts, sifting through layers of ancient rubble, and toiling away in museums and laboratories piecing together tiny fragments of writing left behind on disintegrating scrolls and the broken remnants of storage jars.

What I want to make clear is that I am not one of those people and, more important, that this book could not have been written without them.[1]

Now, this leads me to the second bit of advice. Never having been on an archaeological dig and not knowing any of the languages used during the first century, I've listened and tried to pay attention to what archaeologists, historians, and literary and biblical scholars have to tell us about life in year one, CE.[2] What I quickly discovered is that the people who know the most

---

1. Nor, as you'll see, could this book have been written without the digressions scholars rely on known as "footnotes." Let me explain. First, if you decide to read these notes you'll discover different perspectives and some clarifications on the history being told up there in the main text; this is important, for example, on the few occasions when we're forced to consider two or three (it's unclear) people named Judas all living in Galilee and all possibly having something to do with a revolution; I try to sort out who's who. There are also moments when I find something a scholar says about daily life in first-century Palestine to be a little confusing, flatly wrong, or even offensive; I try to make note of that, as well. A third purpose for the footnotes is to draw connections between life in the first century and life in our own time. Taken together, the footnotes offer a running commentary on the lessons we have and have not learned from our past.

2. "Year one" or "year one, CE" will be a kind of shorthand for us, as this book's title suggests, to mean most of the first century. That said, as I explain in the Introduction that follows, the exact time frame actually begins a few years before year one and does not quite reach the end of the century.

about first-century Palestine tend to repeat the same somewhat frustrating maxim: No one really knows for sure what life back then was like. Frustrating as it may be, this has by necessity become a maxim for *Life in Year One*, as well.

Beyond that limitation, however, scholars have all kinds of theories about first-century Palestine, and I've done my best to present those theories that make the most sense, or are the most interesting, to me. Where I think competing theories each make their own kind of sense or are each of particular interest, I've tried to present all sides as fairly as possible. And so, while I've tried to pay attention to as many people as I could, those I ended up listening to most you'll find mentioned a lot in the notes. The people I listened to only a little you'll see are mentioned less. This is not a value judgment, necessarily. It's just that I find some experts more interesting than others, and often those experts also make more sense to me. But make no mistake: This book is a product of my listening to a wide variety of people and then trying, in the words of a more common translation of Jesus' advice, to understand.

Finally, over the years I've grown to love a particular verse from the book of Ezekiel that sees listening and paying attention a little differently: "O mortal," God tells the prophet, "eat what is offered to you; eat this scroll and go." While I am by no means a prophet like Ezekiel, what God demanded of him seems a little like what happened to me when I came to write this book. I was given a whole lot of scrolls to eat. And today, as I imagine myself sitting around devouring all kinds of books and then writing this one, Jesus' last remark reminds me that it's not what goes in that corrupts us, it's what comes out. In other words, though I've relied on lots of other writers while writing this book, whatever mistakes and missteps I make here are no one's fault but my own.

S.K.

N.Y.C., AUGUST 2009

THIS IS NOT A BOOK ABOUT JESUS

Jesus said this to his disciples, "Compare me; tell me what I am like."
Simon Peter said to him, "You are like a just messenger."
Matthew said to him, "You are like a wise man of philosophy."
Thomas said to him, "Teacher, my mouth is utterly unable to say what you are like."

—*The Gospel of Thomas* 13

This book means to be a lively romp through the land of Palestine as it was in the first century, roughly the time Jesus of Nazareth is supposed to have walked the earth. We want to know what life might have been like back then. But we should also be clear from the beginning: This is not a book about Jesus. Yet, if Jesus had been the kind of person who had neighbors, which by all accounts he very much wasn't, this would be a book about them.

While this means that I don't pretend to be offering an account of Jesus' life story (nor that of anyone else from the first century, in full), for the sake of having some meaningful and somewhat familiar time frame, the exact period we're concerned with begins around 5 BCE,[1] which is believed to be the year Jesus was born.[2] In a sense, Jesus is our way into his world. Every piece of this book, beginning with my Author's Note, starts with his commentary on the world he belonged to (or we'll soon see, maybe didn't belong to). The other end of our timeframe is 70 CE, the year the Romans destroyed Jerusalem's Second Temple, the center of the Jewish world, which basically marked the end of life as they knew it for Jews of Jesus' time.[3]

---

1. BCE stands for Before the Common Era, another way of saying BC, or Before Christ; likewise, CE, an abbreviation we've already seen, stands for Common Era, another way of saying AD, or *Anno Domini*, Medieval Latin for "in the year of our Lord." Obviously one of these sets of abbreviations is a secular way to mark years and the other is a religious way to mark years. In recent time, the secular approach has become more or less standard, especially among people attempting to tell ancient history. I hope I'm being overly cautious when I say that my use of BCE and CE is not meant to offend anyone.

2. In other words, Jesus was not born at the start of year zero, as one might suspect. In fact, looking back, there was no year zero. The Gregorian calendar, in use since 1582, jumps from 1 BCE to 1 CE, which means that the first millennium was already a year old before it was even a day old. This also meant that as 1999 became 2000 you had a lot of know-it-alls at New Year's Eve parties confronting people with the fact that Y2K was really no big deal and that the "actual millennium" would not occur until next year's party, a party to which those same know-it-alls were probably not invited.

3. Given the attachment Jesus expressed even as a child for the place he called "his Father's" (Luke 2:49), or his anger at the money changing that typically went on there to allow Jews to pay their Temple dues (Wills, *What Jesus Meant*, 65), one can only imagine how he might have felt had he lived to see its destruction.

As for the place, geographically, if not religiously or politically, Palestine is still Palestine, Jerusalem is still Jerusalem, Nazareth is still Nazareth, and the region known as Galilee still goes by that name. The Jordan River still connects the Sea of Galilee and the Dead Sea. The ancient port of Caesarea continues to be washed by the Mediterranean (although the Mediterranean was known by Romans as "Our Sea" and by the Jews as the "Great Sea"). And while it may seem safe to assume that claims made on that part of the world have grown especially complicated over the last century, particularly since the 1948 Arab-Israeli War, life was actually no more simple, no more peaceful, in the first century than it is today; even so—and no doubt because—the Holy Land is still the Holy Land.

From what we know about first-century Palestine, my choice of the word "lively" above may be something of an understatement. This was a time of insurgency, banditry, widespread soothsaying and prophecy, political backstabbing and religious uprising, and a good many instances of religious backstabbing and political uprising, all of which, in their own ways, culminated in a war that, by one existing account, left more than a million people dead, most of them Jews.

This war has come down to us as "the war of the Jews against the Romans," or "The Jewish War," thanks to the historian Josephus, who, though Jewish, ended up on the side of Rome and the Empire, which since 63 BCE included the Holy Land. The war ended in 73 CE, just a few years after the destruction of both the Temple and the whole of Jerusalem. (It has not gone without saying, of course, that written from the Jewish perspective the history of this war might have been called "The History of the Roman War against the Jews." But to the victors go both the spoils and, in today's terms, the spin.) And while much of what follows here will deal with the lead-up to the war and the endless troubles both bubbling up and bubbling over between the Romans and the Jews for most of the first century, pausing for a moment here, with Josephus, should allow me to illustrate one more thing we should be clear about.

No one today can tell us unequivocally what it was like to live in this world. Very little that was written back then has survived. And while we're lucky to have the writings of not only Josephus but also the whole New Testament, some other Christian writings, and the work of Philo, a Greek-speaking Jewish scholar from Alexandria, what we can learn about daily life from them is limited. In his writings, for example, Philo wasn't particularly concerned with his own day, but instead with doing what scholarly Jews have always done—that is, interpret the Torah—and also with telling the stories of great Jewish heroes like Abraham and Moses. Practically all the rest of what's come down from that time is the records of the success stories like the rise of Christianity and the powerful victors in war like the Romans. In other words, there was no first-century equivalent of Walker Evans and James Agee's *Let Us Now Praise Famous Men*, a wandering and intimate portrait of the lives of southern sharecroppers and tenant farmers[4] published in 1941. And even

---

4. This reference to a Depression-era book about American sharecroppers and tenant farmers will make more sense as we begin to understand exactly the relationship

acknowledging the usefulness of stories from history's winners, so to speak—for example, we learn a lot from Josephus, himself once a rebel leader, about first-century Jewish terrorists[5] and assassins known as the Sicarii (more on them to come)—we have good reason to be skeptical about any ancient histories that have survived. Let's just look once again at Josephus's final words on the Jewish War. Not known for perfect accuracy and given his allegiance to Rome, inclined to exaggerate, he reports the body count this way: "All the prisoners taken from the beginning to the end of the war totaled 97,000; those who perished in the long siege 1,100,000.[6] Of these the majority were Jews by race." Though he admits not all of those who were killed were citizens of Jerusalem, it's difficult to imagine more than a million people meeting their end in a city whose entire population at the time was probably only between 40,000 and 80,000.

Putting aside any worries we might have about exact accounting, the people affected by the Jewish War, and before that those faced simply with living under Roman rule, are the ones whose lives we're interested in. Those are arguably the same people whose lives were touched by Jesus as we know him from the Gospels. And of course we catch glimpses of these people, and in some cases learn a good deal about them and

---

between Rome and the average Jewish peasant, a first-century sharecropper and tenant farmer.

5. "Or," the editor E. Mary Smallwood notes, "(from the man's own viewpoint) a freedom-fighter." In Josephus, *The Jewish War*, 461.

6. The Roman historian Tacitus counted some 600,000 killed (Tacitus, *Histories* 5.13).

their concerns, as they interact with Jesus during the years of his ministry. So, if what we're trying to do is paint a picture of daily life in the first century, especially the goings-on in those towns and neighborhoods where families were often just looking to make ends meet, why not look directly at Jesus for some answers?

We should, and we will. Not only will sayings of Jesus lead us into every chapter, but new translations from the lowbrow Greek of the New Testament will give us a sense of how people haggling in the marketplace or preaching on a street corner may have sounded. (More on these translations in a moment.)

But if what we're interested in is the life of an average first-century Bethlehemite, or a Nazarene, or a Jewish priest living in Jerusalem, focusing on Jesus strikes me as a bad idea. Because what's clear from any reading of the New Testament and other early Christian writings, and what is just as true for believers and nonbelievers alike, is that Jesus was not your average first-century Galilean. The Gospels couldn't be more clear on this. Asked by Jesus to compare him to something (*anything!*), to tell him what he is like, the apostle Thomas finds himself at a loss: "Teacher, my mouth is utterly unable to say what you are like."[7]

---

7. Not an official book of the New Testament, *The Gospel of Thomas* is a collection of 114 "secret teachings" of Jesus, known only by name until 1945, when an Egyptian peasant stumbled upon a jar buried in the earth while collecting fertilizer near a village called Nag Hammadi. Contained in the jar were thirteen leather-bound manuscripts that had been buried in the fourth century. *The Gospel of Thomas* was among them (Ehrman, 116–17). Scenes like this one, where Jesus questions his followers, can be found in the other Gospels as well, although in his own Gospel, Thomas, believed by some early Christians to be Jesus' twin brother, not surprisingly takes center stage.

He was not like a messenger, he was not like a wise man of philosophy, and he was certainly not like us. It may be, in fact, that understanding the life of a typical person from Jesus' time might mean looking at the life Jesus led and the things he said and imagining just the opposite.

Modern writers often find themselves as tongue-tied as Thomas, and on occasion do Jesus' speechless apostle one better. Take, for example, this explanation from the book *The Humanity of Christ*, by Romano Guardini, who, like Thomas, seems to have some difficulty—even stopping himself midstride a few times to "put it another way"—telling us what Jesus is like:

> If Jesus is a mere man as we are, even though a very profound one, very devout, very pure—no, let us put it another way: the measure of his depth, devotion, purity, reverence, will be the measure in which it is impossible for him to say what he says. . . . The following clear-cut alternative emerges: either he is—not just evil, for that would not adequately describe the case—either he is deranged . . . or he is quite different, deeply and essentially different, from what we are.

It's fair to say that Thomas's own trouble getting the words out shows that he believed the very same thing, that Jesus was deeply and essentially different from what we were in even his time.[8]

---

8. Though many people still do think this way, it's not as common as it once was to believe that Jesus was *absolutely* different from the other people who lived during the first century. He was a peasant. He was a Jew. He was a healer who acted like a rabbi and a prophet. Some people see him as a revolutionary. Many modern writers about

Which leads me to say something now that should help us understand the people this book is concerned with: There is nothing deeply and essentially different between who we are now and who we were then.

In 1962, Catholic novelist Flannery O'Connor introduced the second edition of her book *Wise Blood* with this acknowledgment: "That belief in Christ is to some a matter of life and death has been a stumbling block for readers who would prefer to think it a matter of no great consequence." If the argument that Jesus is not at all like us isn't reason enough to explain why this cannot be a book about him, O'Connor's "stumbling block" analogy gives us another reason, which is just as good.

For an example of the kinds of stumbling blocks that keep us from coming to terms with Jesus, let's take the mystery of his youth and early education, which are mysterious mainly because the Bible says almost nothing about them. One could ask, for example, *Did Jesus, as a child, learn to read and write?*

The simple answer is that we just don't know. For every expert who argues, "it must be assumed that Jesus was by no means uneducated; he was certainly able to read and write," there's another

---

Jesus do what Thomas was incapable of. Their mouths are *utterly able* to say what he is like. As we'll see, the problem is that even if Jesus was not essentially different from his neighbors, today we still can't seem to agree about who he was. (It deserves mention, as well, that people had a hard time coming to an agreement even in his own time—even among the writers of the Gospels.) It's worthy of lively debate, to be sure—just not here.

who claims with equal force, "[h]e was an illiterate peasant, but with an oral brilliance that few of those trained in literate and scribal disciplines can ever attain." (We'll see that illiteracy was basically the rule among first-century peasants.) Even the Bible isn't perfectly clear on the matter. At first glance, the Gospels seem to suggest that growing up Jesus did learn to read and write. After all, the one time we do see him as a child, it's after he's slipped away from his parents. Only three days later do they find him "seated among the scholars, both listening to them and asking them questions. All who heard him were astonished at his intelligence and responses." Presumably, if you're sitting with scholars discussing theology, you probably also know how to read and write. But we can't know for sure, or, in any case, the Bible doesn't say. Jesus might have been both precocious and illiterate.

Later in the Gospels, though, when defending a woman who was caught "in the very act" of adultery, Jesus calmly, coolly even, bends down and draws, or writes, something in the dirt. Catholic writer Garry Wills describes the scene this way: "At first he says nothing, but engages in a prophetic action"—the drawing—and then "he goes to an inner truth," in these familiar words, "Let any one of you who is sinless be the first to stone her." Then Jesus bends over and starts writing again, which is when those accusers take off. Jesus has, as Wills cleverly puts it, "ignored them away." That none of them is sinless seems pretty clear. But on the question of Jesus' literacy, it seems now that the writing is on the wall, so to speak: By writing in the dirt Jesus proves he could write (and, of course, read). Still, Wills reminds us that Jesus "wrote nothing for his followers in a later age." More to the point, when talking about the scene with the adulteress, Wills concludes: "We are not told that he formed words, and if they were important to the story John would presumably indicate what they were. . . . In an oral culture, writing was a less effective response than spoken words, as Socrates maintained. When a prophet makes some symbolic gesture, the *action* is what matters."

Scholars will probably always disagree about whether Jesus could read. As we've seen, even the Bible isn't always clear.[9] At least one expert thinks it doesn't really matter. What this debate reveals, however, is that as soon as any one of us starts talking about Jesus, even concerning something as seemingly uncontroversial as whether the man could read, it's difficult not to get sidetracked, to try to make some sense, or some meaning, out of him. We make claims about Jesus that reflect both how we understand him and how we understand ourselves.

---

9. To be fair, the Bible does seem pretty clear at Luke 4:16, where we find Jesus in the synagogue reading from a scroll containing the prophecies of Isaiah. But bear with me for a moment. There may be a number of reasons to question Luke's story here. We don't, for instance, find the scene in the other Gospels. But what seems even more curious is that in another moment when Jesus quotes the Scriptures— that is, the Psalms, just as he gives up the ghost—he does so in Aramaic and not in Hebrew: *Eloi, eloi, lama sabachthani?* (My God, my God, why have you abandoned me?) (Matthew 27:46; translated by Wills, *What Jesus Meant*, 114.) Now, if Jesus had learned the Scriptures by reading Hebrew scrolls and committing them to memory, why, at the very moment of his death, would he bother to translate the Psalms into the language he spoke with his friends? (More to the point, perhaps, is this: *How* could a man suffering the most excruciating torture imaginable think on his feet like that?) Of course, it's possible that Jesus knew both Hebrew and Aramaic equally well and wrote and read and spoke in both languages. Yet, it remains just as possible that like most other first-century peasants he couldn't read, and as we might expect, at the end, quoting the Scriptures in a language we never see him reading or writing, he dies not in Hebrew, but in Aramaic.

He becomes, in a sense, *our* Jesus. And as Flannery O'Connor reminds us, who *our* Jesus is always matters a great deal—even to scholars. For even as one person decides that questions about his literacy don't really matter, to some other person, the idea that Jesus could read even *this book* might be an article of faith. And though I'd love to imagine Jesus turning these pages or peskily reading over your shoulder, I think it's best if I stop myself here and simply state once again: This is not a book about Jesus.[10]

The common written language of first-century Galilee and Judea, and so, most of the writings that make up the New Testament, was a form of Greek known as *koinē*, which literally means "common" or even "common denominator"—as in *lowest* common denominator. New Testament Greek was the same inelegant language of the marketplace, a "pidgin language," according to Garry Wills, whose ideas about translating the Bible—not to mention his translations themselves—have been very important in bringing that language to life in these pages.

---

10. In that same 1962 introduction to *Wise Blood*, O'Connor ascribes the integrity of her main character, the "blind" street preacher Hazel Motes, to his inability to "get rid of the ragged figure who moves from tree to tree in the back of his mind." That ragged figure, of course, is Jesus, haunting Motes even as he preaches his new religion, "The Church Without Christ." O'Connor goes on: "Does one's integrity ever lie in what he is not able to do? I think that usually it does, for free will does not mean one will, but many wills conflicting in one man." (O'Connor, 5). With our own ragged man haunting these pages, I'd like to think she's right about where our integrity lies.

The detailed answer to the obvious question *Why Greek?* or *Why koinē?* is a complicated one that would have to tell of Alexander the Great's overwhelming military and cultural conquests of the world, which, in fact, took place centuries before the seventy-five years we're dealing with in this book. For our purposes, suffice it to say that as Alexander conquered more lands and more people—from Greece to Egypt and Israel, to India and beyond—his language came with him, and if those people he conquered were to survive in the growing Empire, they would have to learn to communicate not just with those who took charge over them, but also those other foreign people Alexander defeated. And so they learned Greek—and fast. As a result, the language they learned, or rather, fumbled to develop, was not the classical, literary Greek of Homer or Plato or Alexander's teacher Aristotle. It was a practical Greek used throughout Alexander's empire, and maintained under the Roman rule that followed, by diplomats and the military, merchants and their shoppers. In this new Greek, as Wills puts is, "words are strung together . . . to get across a basic meaning."

What Wills has done for me, and what I hope the new translations here will do for you, is to revive thoughts and ideas that have grown dull and commonplace—even meaningless—after centuries of the sanitizing, pious "thees" and "thous" of what we know as "biblical English."[11] What's

---

11. Though highly poetical and now certainly antiquated, there was a time when for some readers the "thees" and "thous" of the King James Bible, the birthplace of biblical English, would have sounded perfectly familiar and not at all formal or sanitized. Self-professed language fanatic Elizabeth Little offers an explanation in her breezy (!)

more, when translated anew, words whose meanings may have always seemed clear or obvious to us—say, "apostle" or "church"—can suddenly take on fresh and illuminating meanings. As Wills notes, "[apostle] was not an office but a function" and "the misunderstanding of this term comes from trying to turn it from a function to an office, and a ruling office at that"—in other words, being an apostle was about *what you did*, not *who you were*. That meaning has been lost. And what has been translated for centuries as "church," the Greek word *ekklēsia*, means nothing more than "gathering," which usually happened at someone's, often a woman's, house. No steeple, no stained glass, no pews, and no organ—that is, no building, no male priest, no church.

It would be impossible to overstate how important Garry Wills has been in determining how and why the words of Jesus get translated the way they do here—in his words, to exhibit their "rough-hewn majesty, an almost brutal linguistic earthiness." Still, I owe the greatest credit for bringing to life that common language to Patrick Stayer, whose brief Translator's Note explains his belief in what he calls the "flexibility and force" of *koinē*.

---

book of linguistics, *Biting the Wax Tadpole*: "The linguistic counterpart to the Quaker belief in plain dress was plain speech, in which everyone, regardless of social standing, was addressed with familiar pronouns to emphasize the fundamental Quaker belief in egalitarianism. At the time, though, the familiar forms were 'thou' and 'thee'" (Little, 162–63). Egalitarianism is something Jesus seems to have believed in (which explains the famously egalitarian Quakers' belief in it), and familiarity and informality are the very heart of *koinē*. Even so, "thee" and "thou" sound very differently to our ears than they might have to a Quaker in the middle of the nineteenth century. And what's important is the impact of our translations today.

Finally, for those of us hoping to say something about the time and place in which Jesus lived, two words in particular can come in very handy. (Scholars of the first century just love them.) The first of these words is *imagine*, as in, "Imagine the standard Mediterranean family with five members: mother and father, married son with his wife, and unmarried daughter, a nuclear extended family all under one roof." Equally common are the words *it's hard to imagine*, as in, "When one looks at the level of sophistication of the art, poetry, and architecture throughout the Roman Empire in the first century, as well as the archaeological, iconographic, and written evidence regarding musical instruments and modes, it's hard to imagine that vocal harmony *never* occurred." In either case, whether picturing a typical first-century family from Nazareth, a "tiny hamlet of Lower Galilee," where we can suppose about 400 people lived, or likewise attempting to recreate for our own time the hymns and chants of Jerusalem's Second Temple Levitical chorus, "the highest level of professional singing for its time and place," what we have to call upon is our imagination.

The other word that comes up again and again is *perhaps*, as, in the words of the historian A. N. Wilson, from his biography *Jesus: A Life*:

> Anything we say about the historical Jesus must be prefaced by the word 'perhaps', and as this narrative progresses, you will find that in order to avoid wearying the reader with repetitious

'perhapses' I take the New Testament more and more on its own terms. . . . I hope that I have not written fiction, but I am aware that strictly speaking we cannot say as much about Jesus as I have said in the final chapters of this book without an infinity of perhaps, perhaps, perhaps.

All of this comes to one point: A book like this depends as much on any reader's willingness and ability to imagine as the writer's perfect command of an elusive history or his ability to say anything definitively. And in that way, the world I describe in this book is as much yours as it is mine—perhaps more so, depending on your imagination.

I

THE WORLD IN YEAR ONE

Give Caesar's things back to Caesar, and give God's things
to God.

—MARK 12:17

We can't even begin talking about real life in first-century Palestine without being perfectly clear from the outset: In 6 CE—after the spectacular death of the Jewish king Herod the Great and the political unrest and revolutionary violence that immediately filled the vacuum of his kingdom—the whole land[1] officially became part of the Roman Empire. Rome's

---

1. Simply talking about this part of the world threatens to tie us in knots. For the most part, we'll be concerned with the regions of Judea in the south, home to Jerusalem and Bethlehem, and Galilee in the north, with towns like Nazareth and Cana and Capernaum and cities like Sepphoris and Tiberias. And given that for thousands of years the land has been known as a puzzle of mountains and valleys, barren deserts

empire had actually been chipping away at the forests and fields, sands and cities of Palestine since 63 BCE, knocking off bits and pieces of Jewish territory and assigning local governors for nearly a quarter century.

In 40 BCE, with the backing of the late Julius Caesar's best friend Mark Antony,[2] Herod, the appointed governor of Galilee, was chosen by the Roman senate as king of the Jews. In the first years of his reign, Herod consolidated all of Palestine under his rule—and so doing, consolidated Rome's interests, as well—eventually seizing Jerusalem as his capital in 37 BCE. By the historian Josephus's account, Herod's final siege of the city showed both an uncharacteristic restraint and the unrelenting brutality that would typify his rule:

> First to be captured was the area round the Temple; then the army poured in and there was frightful carnage everywhere, as the Romans were furious at the length of the siege, and Herod's Jewish soldiers determined that not one opponent should survive. They were massacred by the thousands, crowded together

---

and fertile farmlands, glorious beaches and bustling cities, we'll have to treat various parts of Palestine with as much particularity as possible. To add to all that confusion—in a way that tightens the knot, so to speak, or perhaps the noose—Palestine itself was not known as "Palestine" to most of the people who lived there during the first century. Those people had all kinds of other names for it—the Land of Canaan, the Promised Land, the Holy Land, the Land of Israel, the Land of Judah, and even just *the Land*—names that have, in their own way, also stayed with us for well over two millennia (Daniel-Rops, 4–5). But since what is important here is to get a sense of what it was like to live in that part of the world at that time, which essentially meant to live under foreign rule, we'll be using the same name the foreign rulers used: Palestine.

2. Of "Friends, Romans, countrymen, lend me your ears."

in streets and houses or fleeing to the Sanctuary. No mercy was shown to infants or the aged, or to defenceless women. Although the king sent round imploring them to discriminate, no one stayed his hand, but as if raging mad they vented their fury on every age alike.

While on the one hand Herod's legacy as king would be his historic architectural vision, including the rebuilt, and by all accounts incomparable, Temple in Jerusalem, it's clear that from the earliest days of his reign the king expressed a real penchant for violence, an aspect of his personality that Christians learn as part of the Christmas story: "Herod went to Bethlehem and massacred all the boys of two years of age and under." Even putting aside the legendary massacre of the innocents from the Gospel of Matthew,[3] for evidence of his cruelty we might point out that Herod is said to have once pulled the skin of a hedgehog over a rabbi's head and face—presumably turning the animal inside out and stretching its hide all the way down to the man's chin—blinding him and slicing him up and down. What's more—as if we needed more—suffering from the extreme jealousy and paranoia that characterized his later years and eventually led to a complete mental collapse, Herod one day called for the "instant execution" of his wife Mariamme and

---

3. I say we can put this specific biblical example aside because any questions about whether the events actually happened as Matthew reports are, with respect to Herod's murderousness, profoundly beside the point. In other words, while Josephus, for example, doesn't include the story from Matthew in his histories, the King Herod that he describes was certainly capable of the dark brutality of these killings we read about in the New Testament.

brother-in-law Joseph on nothing more than the suspicion that they'd been having sex. The sordid details are ones the elite of year one might have come to expect from their king.

That said, about the alleged infidelity of his wife, Herod was positively wrong. And the rest of the story is a little more complicated than what we could say about the rabbi and the hedgehog. For starters, Josephus reports the king concocted the affair—and I quote—"during intercourse" with his wife.[4] In what we might imagine to be one of history's more awkward moments of love-making, Mariamme stopped the proceedings at some point to accuse the king of plotting to have her killed—which, it should come as no surprise, is something he had very recently done.

Having been led by his shrewish mother and duplicitous sister to believe that Mariamme was, from a distance, courting the affections of his powerful friend Mark Antony—"a man who was woman-mad and able to get his way by force," says Josephus—Herod had feared that when two men next met, he might just feel the absolute brunt of Antony's force. And so, before his next trip abroad, Herod had secretly instructed Joseph to kill Mariamme if Herod himself were to turn up dead. (Presumably he couldn't stomach the thought of her living on after him to be with Antony.) Joseph, it turns out, spilled the beans, which led Mariamme, while Herod declared his singular love for her upon his return, to exclaim: "And a nice way . . . to show your love for me—giving Joseph instructions to kill me!"

---

4. Now, how would Josephus have known that?

Convinced in that moment that Joseph had let Mariamme in on the secret murder plot only after first seducing her, Herod's uncontrollable jealousy shifted instantly from Mark Antony to his poor, unsuspecting brother-in-law. The rest, as they say, is history, which for Herod often meant "instant execution."[5]

Intriguing as he is, for now we should leave this Herod behind.[6] Because in the end, we have to face the same facts the Jewish king and his Jewish subjects did. The man with the greatest impact on daily life in Palestine throughout the first century was someone far greater than Herod the Great.

We're talking, of course, about the Roman emperor, whatever his name, one in a long line of rulers running from Octavian (a.k.a. Augustus), Julius Caesar's successor, to Vespasian, who wiped Jerusalem completely off the map, including the magnificent Temple, which Herod had built as a testament to his own greatness and, of course, the eternal greatness of his God.

The Roman historian Tacitus tells us that even amid the rubble and the dead of a city ancient Jews had known simply as

---

5. Of course, erratic and borderline crazy as he was, Herod would very quickly live to regret this decision. "So hot was the flame of his desire that he could not believe her dead," writes Josephus, "but in his sickness of mind talked to her as if still alive, until time revealed to him the terrible truth, and filled his heart with grief as passionate as his love had been while she lived" (Josephus, *The Jewish War*, 87).

6. This Herod is not to be confused with his son, Herod Antipas, who left his mark after being installed by Rome as tetrarch of Galilee and a second region called Peraea along the Jordan River. "Tetrarch" is a Greek word originally used to describe the ruler of a quarter piece of a given territory, and it appears to have meant a lot more when used by ancient Greeks than when used by Rome in the first century. Though Antipas was important—and as we'll see, feared—throughout Galilee, the lone encounter we know of between him and the emperor Caligula ends with Antipas being banished to Spain, where he died in total obscurity. More on Antipas to come.

the City, "the common people . . . could not be brought even by disasters to believe the truth." But what exactly was this unbelievable truth? On the one hand, Tacitus meant what must have been perfectly unmistakable—that Jerusalem, their home, and, as they imagined it, the very center of the world, was gone. But an even greater truth Tacitus is getting at has to do with what those common people had refused to believe, in some cases heroically, for decades: The Roman Empire completely ran the show in Palestine during the first century.

We shouldn't imagine that Roman emperors would have showed their faces very much around first-century Palestine—not even on coins, which everywhere else in the Empire were covered in Caesars' "heads." Nor should we imagine tiny peasant villages like Nazareth (pop. 400), say, filled with Roman guards in silver-plated armor and crested helmets knocking on doors and patrolling the streets. Even streets themselves would be assuming too much of a place like Nazareth. It's likely that the average Nazarene or poor fisherman from Capernaum (pop. 600–1,500), a few miles away, would never even have met a Roman.

But rest assured: What the common people probably never saw—and if Tacitus is correct, perhaps never truly believed—they most certainly would have felt in their proverbial pocketbooks. Because despite whatever difficulties we face saying anything definite about life in first-century Palestine,[7] there are

---

7. *Q.v.*, "Introduction: This Is Not a Book About Jesus." And take, for example, the confusion archaeologist Jonathan Reed describes in the introduction to his book, *Archaeology and the Galilean Jesus*: "[I]n terms of ethnicity, [Galilee] has been described as Jewish, 'Israelite,' or even syncrenistic and Gentile; in terms of cultural

two things we can safely say were as certain about the world in year one as they are about our own world: *Death*, of course, and—you guessed it—*taxes*. And given the time and place and peoples we're concerned with, we might say that these two certainties were related. We're talking about something more than the typical grumbles, say, about the unfairness and inexplicability of the U.S. tax code. We'll be interested here in the very special, often revolutionary, ire that comes with paying taxes to a foreign ruler. (Think, for example, about the Boston Tea Party and its aftermath.) Still, it takes years for revolution to steep, and revolution is not all we'll be concerned with. So, for the purposes of our story, let's start with taxes.[8]

---

traditions and religion, Galilee has been portrayed as either conservatively Jewish or Hellenistic; in terms of economics, either impoverished or prosperous; in terms of its political climate, it has been portrayed as either zealously nationalistic or shrewdly acquiescent." All this seems to prove is what I said at the beginning: No one really knows what it was like to live in this world. Yet, one thing all these particular descriptions of Galilee have in common is that they were written to provide a context for a historical Jesus—that is, to see and understand Jesus in a particular way—which is, of course, the very thing we're hoping to avoid. What Reed is also saying, though, is that if we're going to get any sense of what the world is like, we should ask archaeologists for help. Unlike those of us who look specifically to the literary works of the time—works that Reed calls "intentional witnesses from antiquity, whose authors want to tell a story, make a plea, or regulate life"—archaeologists "uncover many unintentional witnesses to life in antiquity in the form of artifacts that make up 'the paraphernalia of everyday life': sherds from pots and pans, hidden coins, discarded kitchen scrap—all afford a glimpse behind closed doors of antiquity" (Reed, 8–9, 19). In other words, if no one knows what it was like to live in first-century Palestine, archaeologists like Reed would say that they don't know *best*. I happen to agree.

8.   Admittedly, descriptions of first-century deaths might make for a more exciting opening chapter than stories about taxes and the people who administered them. But since we're trying to avoid any theological speculation about the afterlife in these pages, I hope you'll agree that starting with ancient taxes actually makes more sense. See, where death is concerned, there will be little more we can say with any certainty after detailing the terrifying and grisly fact of a Roman crucifixion (different from a

A ll was quiet," is how Tacitus described Palestine for the years between 14 and 37 CE. That said, this is, admittedly, an exciting time in the Christian imagination and was anything but quiet for the earliest Christians alternately spreading the word and desperately infighting (most famously about whether new converts had to be circumcised). Even so, Tacitus clearly saw things differently.[9] And what "quiet" would have meant from his Roman perspective was that people seemed to be paying their taxes and not complaining too much about it. And nowhere were the quiet workings of this relationship between your average family and the Empire more clear than in

---

Jewish one, where only a dead person would be put on such gruesome display [Crossan, *The Birth of Christianity*, 523] or the specifics Josephus provides about how King Herod met his end ("unbearable itching all over his body . . . swellings on the feet as in dropsy," and most troubling of all, perhaps, "mortification of the genitals, producing worms" [Josephus, *The Jewish War*, 117]). And so, taxes first, on the theory that there will be no place to go but up. Which is to say we'll get to death later—even those specific, spectacular deaths—where it makes sense, in chapter X, very near the end.

9. Tacitus simply had no reason to be bothered by the birth of Christianity in and of itself. Not until this "class hated for their abominations"—that is, Christians— popped up in Rome and were blamed by the emperor Nero for burning the city in 64 did Tacitus see a need to record any of their history for posterity. Reporting on the fates of those Roman Christians under Nero, Tacitus writes, almost gleefully, "Covered with the skins of beasts, they were torn by dogs and perished, or were nailed to crosses, or were doomed to the flames and burnt, to serve as a nightly illumination, when daylight had expired." It's also in this context that Tacitus notes the "extreme penalty" Jesus faced under Pontius Pilate, the Roman prelate (or, a second-rank governor [Crossan, *Jesus*, 136]). By killing Jesus, Tacitus claims, Pilate "checked for a moment" what was "a most mischievous superstition" (Tacitus, *Annals* 15.44).

the central Galilean city of Sepphoris and the countryside and villages that surrounded it.

In the tumult that followed Herod's death in 4 BCE, a Galilean known as Judas, the son of a bandit chief named Hezekiah, broke into the royal armory at Sepphoris and stirred up an insurrection with the hope of taking the throne himself.[10] In response, at least according to Josephus, the Romans burned Sepphoris to the ground and enslaved its inhabitants,[11]

---

10. Excuse me for this long footnote, but we should be clear about something: This name "Judas" has caused some real confusion among those who read Josephus and the New Testament and try to make sense of the history we find in each. We'll see much later that a revolutionary named Judas the Galilean bucked against Rome in 6 CE, essentially creating a new sect of Judaism that would disrupt relations between the Empire and its subjects in Palestine for the remainder of the century. Josephus doesn't connect the two mentions of Judas, and it's been hard for anyone to say for certain whether he's talking about the same person in both cases. Jonathan Reed has conflated the two (if there were, in fact, two) by suggesting that the reason for Judas's attack on the armory had something to do with paying taxes to Rome, that it "infringed on God's sovereign rule over Israel" (Reed, 100); to be fair, Josephus actually says nothing of the sort, only that in 4 BCE, a guy named Judas, whose father was a bandit, went after Herod's throne. The resistance of Judas the Galilean ten years later, however, did seem concerned with the sovereign rule of God. "In his time," says Josephus, "a Galilean named Judas tried to stir the natives to revolt, saying that they would be cowards if they submitted to paying taxes to the Romans, and after serving God alone accepted human masters" (Josephus, *The Jewish War*, 126, 133). (This Judas's death at the hands of Rome is recorded in the Acts of the Apostles 5:37.) Neither Judas (if, again, there were two) should not be confused with a third Judas from Galilee, Judas Iscariot, who probably came to think about taxes much the same way Jesus did—that is, give back to the emperor what belongs to the emperor and give to God what belongs to God.

11. Reed thinks we might have reason to be skeptical of Josephus's account, noting that there has been "no widespread evidence of destruction" of the kind described in *The Jewish War* and the later work *The Antiquities of the Jews*. "[Josephus's] tendency to exaggerate Roman might and the repercussions of rebellion," says Reed, "must be considered when interpreting this passage." At the same time, though, Reed will admit that whatever the Romans did to Sepphoris after the rebellion by Judas, it seems to

something that would affect the city and the countryside for the duration of the century. And so, when King Herod's son, Herod Antipas, was made tetrarch of Galilee—a Greek title that loosely means "prince," although in the grand scheme of things signifies fairly low status—he would essentially be starting from scratch. Antipas would rebuild Sepphoris from the scorched ground up.

Building a city is expensive, even if you're not striving to live up to the example set by your father, Herod the Great, the greatest Jewish contractor in a millennium. (One also senses a kind of sibling rivalry with half brothers Philip and Archelaus, each likewise awarded pieces of Palestine after their father's death.) And Sepphoris was chosen by Antipas to be, in Josephus's words, the "ornament of all Galilee"—designed in the Greco-Roman style, complete with a main shopping street, known as the *cardo*, that stretched nearly forty-five feet across. By the time things had quieted down throughout Palestine, the population of Sepphoris had soared from around 1,000 to between 8,000 and 12,000 people. And the preferred method to pay for streets paved with sturdy limestone or massive granite columns running along the roofed sidewalks, and still make

---

have left a strong impression throughout Galilee. Sepphoris itself, for example, beginning with the rule of Antipas, would develop and maintain strong ties and allegiances to Rome throughout the first century. On the other hand, to an itinerant rabble-rouser from Nazareth, who knew very well of Herod of Antipas's execution of John the Baptist, and had probably heard stories of Judas's failed uprising, the city would have seemed very dangerous indeed. As Reed concludes, it's no wonder there's no Gospel story of Jesus traveling to Sepphoris (Reed, 117, 137).

sure Rome got its take, had been put in place. The massive basilica with its mosaic floor and frescoed walls, and the modest Roman-style theater carved into a natural cavity in the earth (probably after mid-century), it was all paid for on the backs of the rural poor.

The primary relationship of first-century Palestine was between a city and the countryside that surrounded it. Small villages like Nazareth were *oriented* toward larger cities—in this case, Sepphoris, just over three miles to the north. (The same can be said about the relationship between Tiberias, a city about the size of Sepphoris on the Sea of Galilee, and the local farmers and fishermen who supported it.) As Antipas expanded his city construction projects, encouraging huge growth among the urban populations of Galilee, he faced several problems beyond the basic costs of building cities essentially from nothing. On the one hand, what belonged to the emperor—taxes, taxes, and more taxes—increased right along with an ever expanding tax base. Moreover, this increasing tax base included the administrators of Antipas's government and a class of manufacturers who were all paid from the public coffers. And of course, a growing population of increasingly wealthy people with increasingly lavish lifestyles simply needed more food. These were what we might call the early days of conspicuous consumption.

And so, while the cities expanded, filling up with buildings decorated with frescos and connected by roads lined with paving stones, peasants from the countryside and along the Sea of

Galilee remained peasants: landed farmers and fishermen with boats, laborers who worked for them, artisans and beggars. Yet the world around them was changing—their very way of life, the ground beneath their feet, even the waters floating their boats. Farmers whose whole lives had been built around self-sufficiency and bartering—whose families and the families around them were fed with what they could grow and whose taxes were paid from what was left over—were suddenly faced with a new "monetized" economy. Antipas always paid Rome in precious metals, which meant his subjects would do the same. Suddenly, even peasants needed coins.

Coincidently,[12] the cities needed more land to grow more food—land many peasants had been selling off under the pressure they faced to stay solvent in the new economy. Lucky peasants held on to their scattered fields by joining with other peasants and together growing enough surplus grain to sell in the cities, which would have paid enough to cover their tax bills. Unlucky peasants sold everything and either moved to the city and became day laborers or artisans[13] or started renting the very land they had once owned—planting when it was time to plant, harvesting when it was time to harvest, and ultimately transporting food away from the countryside and into the city where it could be refined, stored, and, of course, eaten.[14]

---

12. Well, not really.

13. In those days, giving up a life as a peasant farmer to become a peasant artisan would have been a step down, not up (Crossan, *The Birth of Christianity*, 155).

14. On the bright side, peasants who no longer owned their land also no longer had to deal directly with Antipas's tax collectors.

What had been for centuries heavily forested land, with just a scattering of fields and uncultivated parcels, became under Antipas the first-century equivalent of what we know today as industrial farmland. A full 97 percent of the arable land in this piece of the Empire was cultivated to feed the ever expanding cities.[15] Typically, in situations like this, where tenant farmers and indentured servants grow food for their landlords' sakes, the top 2 percent of the population consumes as much as 65 percent of what is grown in the fields. What the wealthy land-owners didn't consume—that is, what they stored or strategically hoarded—they would often sell back to the very tenant farmers who grew it, especially when the growing went bad. And what's more, taxes on these peasants combined with typical Jewish biblical tithing[16] would have amounted to between one-third and one-half of everything they grew and everything they sold.

In this arrangement, Rome itself stood to benefit most, of course, followed by an urban Jewish aristocracy and the wealthy elites and landlords. The rural peasants were left out to dry, so to speak—feeling for what might have been the very first time what it was like to be what we know today as *poor*. Before the Romans took control of Palestine, farmers and fishermen hadn't

---

15. As I've said, it wasn't just the countryside that was changing. Fishermen were sold the rights to fish the Sea of Galilee and when they returned to shore would pay the tax collector a piece of their haul (Reed, 165).

16. I say *typical* because—surprise, surprise—no one is positive whether peasants in Galilee would have paid a tithe to the Temple in Jerusalem. As Jonathan Reed has suggested, giving to God what is God's, however, would be an instance of this tithing, in any case (Reed, 89).

really needed money for daily use. They may have sensed that they didn't have much, but what they had was theirs. With the Empire all that changed and what the peasant needed most—Roman coins—often became nearly impossible to get a hold of. Once again, just imagine how this must have felt.[17]

---

17. At this point perhaps more than anywhere else, imagining life in year one is the best we can do. As we've said, there simply is no firsthand account to capture the *feelings* of those exploited farmers (Crossan, *The Birth of Christianity*, 158) who worked the land of Roman Palestine. Although, had there been a reporter living among the tenant farmers, I'd like to think peasant life would have stirred up in him a "resolute, private rebellion" like the "unquenchable, self-damaging, deeply principled, infinitely costly, and ultimately priceless" one we find in the New Deal classic *Let Us Now Praise Famous Men*, which documented in twentieth-century America the same class of landless sharecroppers produced by the first-century urbanization of Galilee. James Agee's writing about the American South possesses qualities entirely lacking in the perfectly unrebellious histories of Josephus or Tacitus; what Agee produced was, in his own words, an "effort . . . to recognize the stature of a portion of *unimagined* existence . . . [and] an independent inquiry into certain normal predicaments of human divinity" (Agee, xii, xiv). The emphasis here—*unimagined*—is mine and suggests something about this book that Agee saw in his: There is some moral bravery in our effort to *imagine* the lives of those Tacitus sees as the quiet "common people," or whom Josephus refers to only when they are, as one historian has put it, "politically menacing" (Goodman, 60). And since there is little we can know for sure about life in the first century, with all this in mind I'll echo something I said at the beginning: Whatever moral bravery it might take to imagine the predicament of a first-century peasant, it's all yours.

II

MONEY IN YEAR ONE

I am telling you the truth: a rich man will hardly get into
the kingdom of heaven. I'll say it again: it is easier for a
camel to enter through a needle's eye than for a rich man
to enter God's kingdom.

—MATTHEW 19:23–24

He called in ten of his slaves, gave each ten silver minas,
and told them "go to work until I come home."

—LUKE 19:13

To a degree the people of Palestine had not known before,
the world in year one—the world of the Empire—was
divided between the haves and the have-nots. (There was little
in between.) And while to this point a farmer in Galilee might
have worked his small fields without any real sense of his place
in the pecking order, the times were changing. Marking that
change was, well, what today we call *change*. For the rich and

the poor alike, money in year one meant the brand-new economy of precious metals brought to you at the behest of Rome by Herod the Great and his successors.[1] Most of the coins used during the first century throughout Galilee, for example, came from the Phoenician city and Roman province of Tyre, now part of Lebanon. That Tyre was Roman is probably most important as far as we're concerned. Roman provinces, of course, struck imperial money. (And these coins literally looked *struck*, or very often *mis-struck*, flattened out along the edges with their designs askew.[2]) A Mediterranean port north of Herod's kingdom, Tyre was at the heart of trade routes for the Empire, closer to Rome itself than Herod's palatial city on the Great Sea, Caesarea Maritima—named, of course, for the emperor. With the construction of cities and the population explosion in Antipas's Galilee, coins of larger denominations, and bearing the Tyrian stamp, began replacing older coins once circulated by the ruling dynasty known as the Hasmoneans, who came to power in the middle of the second century BCE.

The fight for Jewish independence and the rule of the Hasmoneans is described in the biblical books of the Maccabees (1 & 2). Josephus also covers what's known as the Maccabean Revolt in both of his histories, *The Antiquities of the Jews* and *The Jewish War*, where he introduces us to a rebel named Mattathias, the son of a priest named Asamonaeus (from which we get "Hasmonean"). This pre-CE Jewish struggle for independence

---

1. In Galilee, for example, the wake-up call was provided by Herod Antipas.
2. What a coin collector today might call an off-center or a broadstrike error.

against the Seleucids, the Hellenistic empire of Syria, would be inspired and at first led by the revolutionary Mattathias.

What exactly led Mattathias to rise up? According to Josephus, the Seleucids were trying "to force the Jews to break their ancient Law by leaving their babies uncircumcised and sacrificing swine on the altar." Mattathias, who believed it was better "to die for the laws of [his] country than to live . . . ingloriously," responded by rounding up his sons and killing the commander of a local garrison with cleavers.[3]

After Mattathias's death, his son Judas, who took on the nickname "Maccabeus," or "The Hammer," would continue a revolt that led to both Jewish independence and also an alliance with Rome, which, as we now know, would result before long in more of the same: life under foreign rule. As a final word for now on the legacy of the Hasmonean dynasty on first-century Palestine, it's worth pointing out that Herod the Great, whose family was from the land south of Judea known as Idumea, an area seen historically by most Jews as hostile and even by the first century still semi-foreign, joined the royal line with his second marriage, to Mariamme, granddaughter of the Hasmonean king Hyrcanus.

So, the Hasmonean dynasty preceded the reign of Herod the Great and, as it's known, the Herodian dynasty, which lasted for nearly the next hundred years. Coins that survived from the Hasmonean period were used for local everyday purchases—say, for bread—or when offering small donations to buy grain for the

---

3. As if a single cleaver wouldn't have done the job.

destitute. Made of bronze, these coins were called prutarchs, and were not worth very much. (Although you can imagine there was some bittersweet value in spending money that reminded you of a time before the Empire.) Roman coins from Tyre were used for trade, in large cities, mainly (even the small city Sepphoris would have seen hardly any international commerce), and were needed for the annual half-shekel Temple offering.[4] And if the wealthy were going to hoard money just as they often did grain, they were going to hoard silver coins from Tyre.

Even to those people who could make neither heads nor tails of their inscriptions,[5] both the coins you'd collected under the Hasmoneans and those that came with the new imperial stamp could tell stories. And the way these coins moved from hand to hand tells us something broadly about the inner workings of the Empire. Of course, these inner workings may not have always been obvious to everyone involved at the time—or as clear as they may seem to us today—especially among those common people just trying to eke out a living. Remember, most of these people would have been much more comfortable simply bartering with their neighbors than paying rents or lining up

---

4. Again, we can't say with any certainty that peasants—or worse, landless Jews— always contributed each year to the Temple. J. D. Crossan and Jonathan Reed say they tithed "haphazardly" at best, and conclude that this laxity apparently "annoyed the rabbis." Nevertheless, the need for Tyrian coins would explain why moneychangers set up shop along the southern wall of the Temple Mount inside an impressive and imposing building some 900 feet long known as the Royal Stoa (Crossan and Reed, 198–99, 210).

5. As we've seen already and as we'll see again, the vast majority of peasants and even a great number of wealthy people couldn't read. Literacy in general at the start of the first century is estimated at between 3 and 5 percent (Crossan, *Jesus*, 25).

for a wage at the end of the day. But at some level, the story had to have been clear. After all, those tiny villages like Nazareth were *oriented* toward larger cities like Sepphoris or the capital, Tiberias, to the east along the Sea of Galilee. That is, even the meager economy of Nazareth came very quickly to depend on the Empire and its growing cities. At the same time, the economies of those Galilean cities depended on their orientation toward other, even larger, cosmopolitan places like Caesarea Maritima and Tyre, which likewise depended on their own orientation and aspirations toward Rome, the seat not only of power but of all the Empire's riches. Similar networks of cities and towns and villages were spread throughout Roman Palestine—the villages in the countryside surrounding Jerusalem were oriented toward that city, for instance—and you found the same pattern throughout the Empire in general.

The layout of these cities, towns, and villages of Palestine were plotted by archaeologist Ian Hopkins in 1980. And the efficiency and economic advantages that stood behind this sort of government administration are simply remarkable. (The means to such ends, of course, are often dubious, to say the least.) But for the sake of argument consider this: In an April 2009 essay for the *New York Times*, Tom Brokaw, former NBC anchor and author of *The Greatest Generation*, commits what he calls the "heresy" of suggesting that across the United States taxpayers could be saved billions if local governments would consolidate various public responsibilities—and, indeed, government positions like mayor or sheriff or judge—in areas where two or more local governments could been seen to, in a sense, cover the same ground. Quoting one New York county executive, Brokaw notes, "Our system of local government has barely evolved over the past one hundred years and we are still governed by these same *archaic institutions* formed before the invention of the light bulb, telephone, automobile and computer." In the end, Brokaw asks, "Is there any reason beyond local pride to maintain such duplication given the economic and population pressures of our time?"

And yet, way back when, with all eyes on him, the Roman emperor kept local pride in check throughout Palestine (for most of a century, at least), and compared with modern-day America, he ran an impressively tight ship—something that is significantly easier to do when you are the emperor.

And finally, while the basic orientation of Palestine toward Rome cannot be overstated, and the aspirations and deference among the elite ran high, we see everywhere that the longings of a city to be like Rome—in language and culture, architecture and, yes, coins—faded as Rome itself faded away into the distance. In other words, the smaller your town and the plainer and more humble your surroundings, the fewer direct interactions you had with representatives of the Empire and the less you handled its currency. And it's hard to imagine someone within the Empire who felt further away from the wealth and culture and power of Rome than a humiliated former landowner begging for the grains he once raised himself or a peasant in Nazareth waking up once again with his head on a rock. Yet for them it was impossible not to feel the Empire even as it faded from view, in large part because they understood that the rocks they slept on and the land they farmed were no longer really theirs.

What they had instead were a few coins.

But odd as this may seem, on one level all was not lost when Rome first came to town. As bad as it was to lose all that once belonged to you, or pay through the nose to keep it, even worse would have been to get the sense that neither the land nor the rock belonged to God anymore, either. After all, it was the God of the Torah who had created everything in the first place. And there was something about a silver half-shekel and even a bronze prutarch that told a different story about first-century Palestine than the one about an empire's fortunes and a peasant's misfortunes.

Indeed, if the first story money told was that Rome had taken charge of Palestine, the second story it tells is about the endurance of God, the keeper and protector of those the Empire had all but completely wrested of their land. Though coins were small and often scarce, for our purposes, the money used throughout Palestine stands as what archaeologists identify as one of only a few perfectly unambiguous signposts leading us through life in the first century. In other words, with first-century coins we can finally know one thing for certain about life in year one: Palestine was the Holy Land, and the people who lived there were Jews.

How can we know this for sure? Because the coins that remain from first-century Palestine are almost entirely[6] what

---

6. *almost entirely*: And exceptions, as they say, prove rules.

scholars call *aniconic*—a word that comes from the Greek suffix *an-*, meaning "not," and *icon*, meaning "likeness," "image," or "portrait." Simply put: no images. From Galilee to Judea, among the priests as well as the prostitutes, from Herod the Great and Herod Antipas to a beggar on Sepphoris's bustling *cardo*, any money exchanged was free of the kinds of images you would have found on coins almost everywhere else in the ancient Mediterranean and that we still find commonplace today, even in Israel. As I've said before: no "heads." Not even any animals. And what this tells us is something we'll see again and again: Through daily humiliations and in defiance of an increasingly violent hand of Caesar, the inhabitants of Roman Palestine kept and protected the God of their fathers by keeping and protecting the Law.

The coins of first-century Palestine fit within an entire society that was aniconic. The pattern was probably begun by the Hasmoneans, who believed the Jewish law against graven images, right there in the Second Commandment, required it. So the story that the coins themselves tell is that even if they were made *by* Romans, they were made *for* Jews. Moreover, on a very basic level, the coins you used—stamped with designs from everyday, palm trees or barley corn or a double cornucopia—told you that you were Jewish and that you led a distinctly Jewish life.[7] It might

---

7. The famous moment from the Gospels where Jesus asks to see a coin and then poses the question of whose likeness appears on it would seem to dispute this claim about this aniconic society (Mark 12:13–17, Matthew 22:15–22, Luke 20:19–26). Direct taxes to Rome, though, which is what he was asked about, would have been paid with coins bearing the likeness of the emperor—in this case, Tiberius, whose

also have told you that you were being tolerated, if not respected, by Rome. Which are, of course, the very same things those coins tell *us* about those people. And it also raises a point that should become even more obvious as we proceed (a point I'm by no means the first to make): You cannot separate the lives of the people of this land from their belief in the God who put them there. More to the point, you cannot separate the lives of the people of this land from their belief *that* God had put them there.

I t should be clear already that coming to these basic conclusions about a land, its inhabitants, and their God should not lead us to imagine simple, uncomplicated lives of a perfectly unified people who all believed and valued the same things.[8] We've given details about how various Jewish groups—from kings to governors, landowners to peasants—dealt with the ruling power of Rome. We've also seen, in part, that Greek

---

coin, showing not only a face but also claiming that Tiberius's father Augustus was *"divi filius,"* son of a divine one (Crossan and Reed, 136), would have been doubly insulting to any first-century Jew. And all this said, a Roman coin serving Roman purposes—and notably not in the possession of the Jew we're talking about—is not the exception that proves the rule.

8. It's almost too obvious to point out that the same could be said of Israeli Jews today. *New York Times* columnist David Brooks takes this a step further, arguing that what actually holds Israelis together today is "argument" itself. And this is no insult. "Israel," Brooks goes on, "is the most diverse small country imaginable. Nonetheless, I may be interviewing a left-wing artist in Tel Aviv or a right-wing settler in Hebron, and I can be highly confident that they will have a few things in common: an intense sense of national mission, a hunger for emotionally significant moments, an inability to read social signals when I try to suggest that I really don't want them to harangue me about moving here and adopting their lifestyle" (Brooks, April 16, 2009).

language and culture continued to leave its mark, more heavily on some than others, on the world we're traveling through.

But admitting all this, we can at least say we know the three most important pieces of the puzzle that was first-century Palestine: Judaism in all its varieties, the Roman Empire in all its power, and Greek culture in all its expressions. And a quick look at the marketplace—or the Greek *agora*, as it was known—should help shed some more light on the situation. At the same time, it should also remind us just how much a fool's errand it would be to try to figure out exactly where the Jewish piece of our story ended and the Greek part began, or where the Greek piece ended and the Roman part began, or where the Roman piece ended and the Jewish part began once again.[9] By year one, Roman Palestine was a snake eating its own tail. Which meant that someone was always getting bitten.

Even in those years the Roman historian Tacitus called "quiet," daily life in the *agora* would have been loud and in some cases might have seemed totally incomprehensible, like Babel itself. Language barriers between speakers of Greek and Latin, Hebrew and Aramaic, would have required sometimes very difficult, sometimes tense, negotiations across a vendor's stall. What's more, even if you shared a spoken language with the person selling you olive oil, or you somehow managed to string together enough words in *koinē* to make your meaning clear, there's still the real chance that the Greek letters on the side of

---

9. It makes you wonder whether Saint Paul was just more or less telling it as it was when he said there was no more Jew or Greek (Galatians 3:28).

a first-century Jew? What could they say to a first-
ian? And what do they teach us?

t with some coins we'd recognize, both minted at
he Jewish revolt in 66 CE, although in two different
stine. And while both these coins are recognizable
of images, it seems for once that to fully appreciate
ritten on the coins you had to know how to read.[14]
inted for an audience we haven't considered so far.
e southern city of Jerusalem and the northern city
respectively, the new coins were made *by* Jews *for*
d though equally aniconic, they couldn't have been
it.

d-up to the devastation of year 70, coins struck in
ok the idea of "Year One" quite literally. Indeed,
ell another story altogether—that of the war itself
discuss later). By the second year of the revolt
Romans, the Jews had decided to start over from
nning of time. In Jerusalem, people were exchang-
hat announced a new creation.[15] Archaeologists
coins stamped with "Year Two/The Freedom of
Three/The Freedom of Zion," and "Year Four/The

---

we're going to be fair, we can probably assume that by year 70, as
to the ground, even the illiterate of that city would have gotten the
ins had been trying to say. Coins minted in Sepphoris in the same
even have reached the illiterate of the city or the countryside, who
content with their bronze prutarchs—perhaps more so then than at
t in their lives.

cal pride.

---

the weight, which spelled out the Latin measure of a half *litra*, would have struck you as utter nonsense.[10] This fact alone could have put you at a considerable disadvantage while haggling over the price of a certain measure of oil.

Or, say you're the guy selling the olive oil—and we should assume men, not women, were doing the selling—and you've arrived at the *agora* manager's booth to pay the taxes on your stall, in oil, as you've agreed. You pour your oil into the storage jar that bears the man's title in Hebrew: *'pmlsh*. And although you're a Hebrew speaker yourself—in fact, one of the rare literate venders in the whole market—for a moment, the Hebrew word is, to use some modern slang, completely Greek to you. Why? Because it's also literally Greek, a Hebrew translation of the word *epimeletes*, which means "manager, overseer, or treasurer." Consider that your Greek lesson for today. And it was an important one, like learning the word *agoranomoi*, or market inspectors, whose job it was to enforce fair business practices in whatever language you had at your disposal, selling permits, handling quality control, and making sure the weights you used were standard.

For all the dissonance it created, the variety of languages that echoed through the colonnaded market street in Sepphoris would have settled into a kind of rhythm of buying and selling, bartering, and no doubt a swindle or two. And if we can take for granted that how we express ourselves bears at least a

---

10. (Greek letters and a Latin measure? It's practically nonsense even today.)

little on what we believe,[11] within that din was as wide a variety of beliefs as there were languages spoken, approximated, or altogether butchered. As J. D. Crossan and Jonathan Reed have said, Judaism has never been "univocal" or "monolithic"; indeed, even in year one, the religion was already known most basically as "ancient and traditional." And traditionally, there has been no single way to be a Jew. And most people of the first century would have taken this idea for granted, even as they handed each other coins that, as we've said, told them that somehow, despite their differences, they were all still Jews.

They would have known that story of Babel from the book of Genesis where God, worried that people might build a tower reaching the heavens, stopped the construction by "confus[ing] the language of all the earth" and then "scattered them abroad over the face of the earth." In the Torah, those were all God's people, fellow Jews, scattered around the world. They were made to speak different languages to safeguard against too much local pride. The babble of Sepphoris, or any of the other commercial cities of Roman Palestine, for that matter, would have reinforced the divine purpose, and the quintessentially Jewish practice—to turn a phrase—of believing what we say.

Of course God's demolition at Babel created, in their minds, not only the relationship between what we say and what we believe, but also the often more troubling fact that the way other people

---

11. That it somehow makes sense to us today that Eskimos could have, and at last count, some 100 words for "snow" tells me that we do take for granted a relationship between the words we use and what we believe in ("There's Snow Synonym," *New York Times*, February 9, 1984).

talk affects what we believe about them. And in the first-century marketplace of Sepphoris, it mattered whether you used Aramaic words, Greek words, Latin words, or Hebrew words—or some pidgin combination of your own devising. Just as a place like Nazareth would have shown hardly any Greco-Roman influence in its appearance, a villager who traveled to Sepphoris or Tiberias to sell his family's surplus or to buy goods he couldn't barter off a neighbor, probably spoke using words he would be judged by.[12] Aramaic almost certainly meant peasant. Hebrew, but no Greek, undoubtedly meant something else, perhaps simply that the Greek-speaker, and certainly the man who could write in Greek, would be your manager. And despite whatever language our olive oil salesman may have picked up while paying his taxes or having his weights inspected, learning just whom he answered to was the greater lesson he learned from the *agoranomoi*[13] and the *'pmlsh* during those quiet, cacophonous years in markets of Roman Palestine.

But as we know, things were not always so quiet. Which raises one final question. What stories did coins struck in times

---

12. Radio spots for the Verbal Advantage vocabulary building program, ads that David Foster Wallace describes as "extremely ominous and intimidating" (Wallace, 96), seem to be getting at an ageless problem: *People judge you by the words you use.*

13. One last thing about these inspectors: The names archaeologists have found in Sepphoris to be associated with the job title *agoranomoi* are Justus and Simeon, both Jewish, as we would expect, and were found written on one side of a lead weight (the same weight, in fact, that shows the Latin measurement of a half *litra* on the other side). What's significant about those names, though, is that they're written in Greek letters (Crossan and Reed, 64–65). Taken together, the Jewish names, Latin measure, and Greek writing on this single weight remind us that, yes, Jews held administrative roles in the Roman economy, but the ones who did were as distinctly Greek as they were distinctly Jewish, which is to say, not distinct at all.

of unrest tell a first-century Jew? What could they say to a first-century Roman? And what do they teach us?

Let's start with some coins we'd recognize, both minted at the time of the Jewish revolt in 66 CE, although in two different parts of Palestine. And while both these coins are recognizable for their lack of images, it seems for once that to fully appreciate the stories written on the coins you had to know how to read.[14] They were minted for an audience we haven't considered so far. Struck in the southern city of Jerusalem and the northern city of Sepphoris, respectively, the new coins were made *by* Jews *for* Romans. And though equally aniconic, they couldn't have been more different.

In the lead-up to the devastation of year 70, coins struck in Jerusalem took the idea of "Year One" quite literally. Indeed, those coins tell another story altogether—that of the war itself (which we'll discuss later). By the second year of the revolt against the Romans, the Jews had decided to start over from the very beginning of time. In Jerusalem, people were exchanging money that announced a new creation.[15] Archaeologists have found coins stamped with "Year Two/The Freedom of Zion," "Year Three/The Freedom of Zion," and "Year Four/The

---

14. Although, if we're going to be fair, we can probably assume that by year 70, as Jerusalem burned to the ground, even the illiterate of that city would have gotten the gist of what the coins had been trying to say. Coins minted in Sepphoris in the same years might never even have reached the illiterate of the city or the countryside, who would have been content with their bronze prutarchs—perhaps more so then than at any other moment in their lives.

15. Talk about local pride.

Redemption of Zion."[16] These were the coins of what Josephus would call the Jewish War. Of course, an inscription minted in "Year One" might have seemed like a concession to another devastating year to follow, so it stands to reason that they may have begun striking coins in "Year Two." (In any case, no "Year One" coins have been discovered.) And ultimately, during "Year Four," which saw the destruction of Jerusalem, it became perfectly clear that there would never be a "Year Five."

By the time "Year Three" had come to Jerusalem, aristocrats and administrators responsible for minting coins in the northern city of Sepphoris had decided to take a different tack altogether, which made sense; it was an approach to Rome that had worked for them for fifty-odd years, ever since Antipas had built the city on ashes left behind by the Empire.[17] With these coins, Sepphoris would declare peace with Rome, not war. And yet, the message sent by the inscriptions seem a little over the top. On one side, the coin says "Caesar Nero Claudius"—the name of the emperor—and on the other side it reads, "Under Vespasian, in Eirenopolis—Neronias—Sepphoris." That is: another reference

---

16. Herod the Great had done something similar at the beginning of his reign as King of the Jews, stamping his own coins with Greek inscriptions reading "Year 3." That said, he qualified the declaration slightly by adding "*Of Herod the King*" (Levine, *Jerusalem*, 174. Emphasis mine).

17. Again, we have to be careful how seriously we take Josephus's reports about the devastation brought to Sepphoris at the start of the century; there's almost no archaeological evidence of the destruction of the city, and Josephus was known to exaggerate the brute strength of Rome (Reed, 117)—something Rome hardly needed. Even so, there's no question that as tetrarch Antipas did all he could to win the favor of Rome and that the same pattern continued throughout the rest of the century.

to a Roman leader—Vespasian would become emperor the following year—and two brand-new names for the city, one Greek, *Eirenopolis*, which means "City of Peace," and then *Neronias*, again, for the emperor Nero. Coins struck the following year followed the same pattern typical of other Jewish coins—again, no images—only in this case, they included a reference to the Roman Senate in addition to name-dropping the emperor: "S" and "C" appear in large Latin letters, which stood for "Senatus Consulto," or "by the decree of the Roman Senate." It's no wonder Josephus remembers Sepphoris in his histories as "the strongest city in Galilee" and home to "the only people . . . who desired peace." All that writing—from the city's Jewish coins to the books of history—was telling essentially the same story, and it was, as we've come to expect, oriented toward Rome.

As a coda, let's ask, What of a final coin, one we wouldn't recognize, minted at another moment of unrest in the Empire? Here is the exception that proves the rule. Coins in first-century Palestine were aniconic, in most cases struck *by* Rome and *for* the Jewish people. They let you know that you were Jewish. Even those coins that seem like exceptions—say, a declaration of peace made in a renamed "City of Peace"—were, for all intents and purposes, as Jewish as anything struck during the Hasmonean dynasty, and, in the case of Sepphoris, were even made of the same material: bronze.

So what was Herod the Great, King of the Jews, thinking when he minted a series of coins showing the likeness of an eagle? This same image, we'll see, appeared at some point on the face of the Temple itself, in what Crossan and Reed consider an "unambiguous symbol of submission to Rome." Their conclusion certainly makes sense for the statue and would make just as much sense for the coins, given all we've said about Palestine's orientation toward Rome. But where Herod was concerned the gesture doesn't seem completely necessary.[18]

I like to think that Herod had simply lost his mind—lost his religion, so to speak—when he decided to mint the coins. Which could also explain why he installed the golden eagle on the Temple. And when death came for Herod, it certainly came like God, with a vengeance. Herod responded in kind. His gestures have been described as "defiant," and they clearly were that. Herod defied his God. But it's the "rage and turmoil" that graven images would arouse in the people that seem of most concern to historians and archaeologists like Lee Levine, who first suggested to me both a relationship between the coins and the eagle statue and that Herod's producing these images at all might mean that at the end of his life he had simply gone insane.

But that said, the story the eagle coins tells me is the story of one man. It is not, for once, the story of a people. Herod was the exception; his coins prove the rule. Roman Palestine was the

18. Crossan and Reed make the case that the eagle would have been located on a piece of the Temple's edifice that was out of the view of Jerusalem's masses and could not be seen from within the Temple itself. On the other hand, it would have been visible to Roman dignitaries approaching from the king's own palaces, and would have served as a reminder to them that with this Temple he had not, in fact, created the "impregnable fortress" it appeared to be (Crossan and Reed, 200).

land of the Jewish God. Their coins told them that, and they tell us the very same thing. In the end, sick and crazed, Herod was bent on defying God, not the people of his kingdom. And while he may have been king to the end, when he minted those coins and cast that golden eagle, he essentially gave up being King of the Jews.

III

HOME IN YEAR ONE

If someone comes to me and he does not hate his father
and mother, wife and children, brothers and sisters—even
his life—he cannot be my disciple.

—LUKE 14:26

No one lights a lamp to set it in secret or under a basket,
but on a lampstand, so people coming in see the light.

—LUKE 11:33

Considering everything going on outside in the world—
what with Rome assuming power, cities like Sepphoris
popping up, and coins from Tyre starting to flow as the life-
blood of a new and expanding economy—we just haven't had a
chance yet to stop and look around at the houses and homes of
the families we've been trying to meet. It's about time we do.

Today, it's often said that the difference between a house
and a home is the difference between a place and the feeling

that place gives you. It's not a perfect distinction, but if you think about it, we buy house paint and enjoy the comfort of home cooking, we do housework[1] and prefer things homemade, and we construct housing developments and develop something called homesickness. And indeed, our ability to imagine life in year one requires that we acknowledge there was a difference between *house* and *home* back then, too. For some people in the first century CE, it was more important what your house said about you, while for others what mattered most was the sturdiness of the foundation of your home—even if the house itself was constructed from rough fieldstones and smeared with mud.

That said, given these important distinctions we might consider the "homelessness" of a beggar in Sepphoris to be something of a misnomer; after all, when we say "homeless" we tend to imagine someone who has no place to go. In first-century Palestine, though, the instability of the family would have caused more distress than losing the building your family lived in[2]—

---

1. Now it's true, we also do something called homework (akin to what we call home-schooling—also aptly named). But homework, like homeschooling, is a part of the development of the individual. Together, individuals make up a family, and it's the family itself that generates—for better or worse—the feeling we associate with home. Today that feeling might ideally be captured in: *Home is where the heart is. Home sweet home. There's no place like home.* Etc., etc. In the first century, though, the motto was simply this: *Father knows best.* (In Greek, the home, or household, was called the *oikos*—Greek had no word for "family" [Ermatinger, 108]—and the one wearing the pants was known as the *oikodespotes.* Look carefully and you should see two words here—*oiko* + *despotes* = home despot [Daniel-Rops, 126]—which should give you a sense of what people thought of good ol' Dad in the first century.)

2. Although if you really stop to think about it, this is probably the way we truly imagine homelessness today, too, in terms of the instability of the whole life, not just the living situation. It's just often the easiest thing to see, and the most obvious thing

although the two might have gone hand in hand. And by distress, of course we're not talking exclusively, or even primarily, about emotions here. Although we should also assume that emotional lives back then would have been no less rich than the ones we enjoy, or just as often don't, today.

One risk we take in talking about homes filled with families is to sentimentalize life in the first century. And sure, there's no reason to think families wouldn't have wished each other "good night," say, before going to sleep. No matter how tough the going may be, routine and the occasional pleasantry, to say nothing of genuine affection, are often the very things that make a household run. And a running household is the very thing we're trying to explore here, as accurately as possible.

Let's consider the first-century family from another, perhaps slightly less sentimental angle, knowing well, as J. D. Crossan has put it, that the home "is not just a center of domestic serenity."[3] What's perhaps more important to understand about day-to-day life in the first century is that despite the buying and selling that went on in the cities and whatever bartering went on throughout the countryside, the basic unit of the economy in first-century Palestine was not the marketplace, but the family.

The size of your family would have been seen as an

---

to say, that what the homeless person is missing is a house, when, in fact, his distress very likely goes much deeper than that.

3.   Basically, Crossan wants to remind us that while home is where the heart is, it's also just as often where the hatred is (to borrow a phrase from soul singer Gil Scott-Heron). "The family is society in miniature," says Crossan, "the place where we first and most deeply learn how to love and be loved, hate and be hated, help and be helped, abuse and be abused" (Crossan, *Jesus*, 60).

economic decision[4] more than one you made as a couple in terms that would suit a romantic notion of your love of children or, as often seems more to the point today, your parents' love of grandchildren. As another historian of the first century tells us, "A common pun turned the word *banim*, children, into *bonim*, builders."

Family planning, in other words, was not born with Planned Parenthood. Although in a time when children were jokingly referred to as builders and fathers were often referred to as "lord," family planning would have meant something different— though not entirely—than it does today. In essence, what it involved was striking an often difficult balance.[5] Families that were too small might not be able to produce or earn enough to live on, either now or in the future; ones that grew too large would risk overextending what were already often meager resources. In a world where social mobility was almost entirely unheard of,[6] the best a father could hope for was balance: the right number of sons to work the fields while he was alive, but not so many that when he died he'd spread the inheritances too thin; and the right number of girls to take care of domestic

---

4. Or, it was a decision in the way that scoring twenty-one in a game of blackjack is a decision.

5. Some would argue—say, like President Barack Obama in his much-talked-about 2009 commencement speech at Notre Dame—that this is precisely what the current debate over family planning requires, some careful and thoughtful balance.

6. Social mobility of the bootstraps variety is as thoroughly modern an idea as family planning is an ancient one. Where social classes were concerned, if you moved in ancient Palestine you almost always moved down. And you would bring your whole family down with you (Crossan and Reed, 20).

work[7] while he and the boys were out in the fields, but not so many that you couldn't pay the dowries to get them all married. An unmarried daughter could be a drain on a family, and the only alternatives for her, in the words of Crossan and Reed, were to "beg or whore."[8]

It might go without saying, then, that in general, boys were much more valued than girls. Girls, after all, grew up to be women, and women, at least by one account, were naturally and, presumably without exception, unfaithful.[9] And be assured, the people who believed this back then were considered the most pious men of their day.[10] On the one hand, we could point to the society's baseline misogyny for the popularity of such an

---

7. But one could probably ask, in a society comprising about 75 percent farmers (Ermatinger, 110), what isn't domestic work?

8. According to Elaine Goodfriend, writing in the popular *Anchor Bible Dictionary*, prostitution was tolerated among Jews in ancient times, which may come as no surprise to us, given the popular understanding of what Mary Magdalene did for a living. (The Bible itself actually says nothing of the sort about Mary.) I have to say, though, that Oded Borowski's suggestion that prostitution was tolerated "to provide an outlet for sexual desire that could not be fulfilled within the prescribed norms" (Borowski, 81) seems to miss the forest for the tree. Why tolerate prostitution? It's the economy, stupid.

9. As Géza Vermes, author of *Jesus the Jew*, points out, this attitude about women seems tame compared with the outright paranoia of the Jewish philosopher Philo of Alexandria: "Women are selfish, excessively jealous, skillful in ensnaring the morals of a spouse and seducing him by endless charms. . . . The husband, bound by his wife's spells, or anxious for his children . . . is no more the same towards the others, but unknown to himself he becomes a different man, a slave instead of a freeman" (quoted in Vermes, 100, 246).

10. Religious piety, in this case, should not be misunderstood for moral consistency— especially between the sexes. Indeed, we can assume that the economic necessity of first-century prostitution demanded a good deal of *unfaithfulness* on the part of many married men. And yet, as we've just seen, this same unfaithfulness in women was known to be their essential flaw. Let's call this a case of moral relativism in year one.

idea, and such pointing might make a good deal of sense even today.[11] Where a father and his family were concerned, however, the preference for sons might have been a simpler matter: Down the road a boy could both earn you more and cost you less. The fallout of this sort of thinking was widespread—both ritually and in the popular imagination. For instance, a woman who gave birth to a daughter would have been considered ritually unclean twice as long as if she'd had a son—eighty days, not the usual forty. Reflecting what was undoubtedly a first-century sentiment, one rabbi remarks in the Talmud, "Girls are but an illusory treasure," admitting at least some good, but then continues, "besides, they have to be watched continually." And then there's the ancient story of one mother, who after giving birth to her fourth daughter named the girl Zaoulé, or "nuisance," and after number eight had simply had it, naming her Tamam, which translates as "That is enough!" That's right—eight is enough.

Sex itself, what we might consider the ways and means of first-century family planning, was tricky business. Of course, it was still done the same way as we do it now, although perhaps without all the modern-day bells and whistles.[12] And by and large,

---

11. Indeed, it was not so long ago that—without batting or rolling his eyes—Henri Daniel-Rops could say this about the "wonderful picture" the Bible paints of the "model for the nation's women": "And everybody knows the poetical description of the good woman before God, with which the Book of Proverbs ends, the woman whose price is beyond pearls, and who brings her husband happiness and knows how to gain his love, who spins, cooks, watches the lamp, works day and night and yet dresses well and helps her husband in his social duties" (Daniel-Rops, 131–32).

12. And also without any acknowledgment, it seems, that women, like men, have what today we euphemistically call *needs*.

sex was encouraged, especially where the plan for the family was to have children (which was almost always the plan). You'll even find at the very end of the first century two rabbis who compare intentional celibacy (of men, of course) to murder.[13] And as we might expect, contraception was officially frowned upon in the first century. Men especially had reason to think the punishment could be great. Consider Onan, from the book of Genesis, who was killed by God not for masturbating, as is commonly believed today, but rather for *coitus interruptus*—a.k.a. pulling out in order to avoid getting a woman pregnant. The distinction, it seems, wouldn't have mattered much in God's eyes, anyway. If you were caught (*caught!?*), both crimes would have been punishable by death—as with any violation of the Law.

But still, people carried on. And where onanism failed or where men lacked nerve in the face of God (fearing God's wrath if they were personally responsible for preventing a pregnancy), women might be called upon to apply topical solutions or what one contemporary author has squeamishly called "inserted preparations," both designed to "block fertilization." Oral contraception, which like magic spells or any other sort of anti-fertilization "preparations," was cooked up without the benefit of actual reproductive science and would hardly have had the desired effect. The rhythm method was, at best, a modest success in preventing families from growing too large. And while abortions were almost universally prohibited, that's not to say they did not exist.

---

13. And not to leave women out of the equation of sex and death, you'll find that at least once the Bible associates barrenness with just being dead (Genesis 30:1).

In any event, infant mortality rates were high in the first century, and if your children lived past infancy, they still had to make it through childhood. About half of all people did not.

Those are, to a certain extent, the conditions within which a husband and wife would have planned their family. How they got to know each other or be married in the first place is, in some ways, slightly less complicated—although hardly less *planned*.

Arranged marriages were the rule of the day, and it should come as no surprise that they were usually the handiwork of the groom's father. (Thanks, Dad.) In other cases a family might hire a matchmaker, although that would hardly have been necessary in the tinier and somewhat isolated villages of Galilee, say, where everybody would have known everybody else. And where likely candidates—ideally, a cousin[14]—would probably have been fairly obvious, given the small number of marriageable women (girls, really) a father had to choose from when the time was right for his son.

Marriages themselves were understood, in large part, as business transactions, or at the very least an arrangement where skills of negotiation would have benefitted a family well.[15] Before a couple could get to the business of planning a family, they first had to get the issue of inheritances, the value of the girl, and

---

14. Marrying your cousin would have simply meant less risk of losing property to another family, and so, as we'll see, easier negotiations of the marriage contract.

15. Sounds romantic, doesn't it?

the dowry out of the way. The marriage contract itself, known as the *ketubah*, became a kind of pre-nup settled between families that would provide assurances not in the case of divorce, primarily—although that was part of the deal—but simply to make sure that the arrangement being made would benefit both families, both now and in the future. First they decided on what was known as the "bride price," an amount, as the name suggests, equal to the value of the bride. (It's unclear exactly how the families would arrive at a number—or if the girl was privy to the negotiations, or ever learned how much she was worth—but it calls to mind the not completely dissimilar business transaction known today as the mail-order, or "business," marriage. In both cases, there is some money to be made, often at someone's expense, if not peril.) In any case, the groom's father put up the money for the girl, unless the groom himself was old enough and could afford to pay for his own bride.

The families would then agree on the dowry, the "gift" paid by the father of the bride to the groom. It represented part of the girl's inheritance and was mainly made up of what are known as movables, things like clothing, furniture, or kitchen utensils—things she would have made use of in the household anyway.

Now, on the one hand, the dowry could be seen as a fee paid to the groom for taking over the responsibility of someone's daughter, who, recall, not only began life by disappointing her parents—*Why can't you be more like your* brother?—but would have begun to cause them actual hardship if they continued to have to feed her, and embarrassment if she left home to . . . well, again, to either beg or whore. But on the other hand, as Professor James Ermatinger points out,[16] because the dowry was given as part of the girl's inheritance, it could be seen primarily as a means of protecting her in case something happened to her husband, which wouldn't have been unusual at all in those days. In other words, the marriage contract may have stipulated that a dowry could be returned to the bride if the husband died or if they were divorced.

Which now brings us, of course, to a few words on what happened when a marriage, for whatever reason, ended.

The death of a husband was a fairly simple problem for a wife (if we ignore whatever emotional attachment she had developed, which, despite all we've said about the business side of marriage, should not be underestimated.[17]) Simply put, if the couple had no son, Jewish law required that his brother marry the widow, unless he was already married himself. (The levirate law, as it's known, and as you may know, has survived into modern times.) And while we shouldn't assume that this happened in every case, the daughters (if they had any) and the dowry would travel with her to the new household. If the deceased didn't have a brother, or presumably if she already had a son, the widow may have returned to live with her family—much, we can assume, to her father's chagrin—or more likely, would have lived on her own, with the eldest son and other children

---

16. And it should be noted that Ermatinger points out a lot of what I'm saying here, even mentioning the similarity between the first-century marriage contract and a prenuptial agreement.

17. In fact, the degree to which couples married for love was probably inversely proportional to how much money they had, which from our perspective perhaps suggests the only benefit of being poor: You got to marry someone you loved (Ermatinger, 104).

helping to support her. If her dowry was large enough, a widow might live well all on her own. But, as Raymond Westbrook reminds us, this doesn't seem to have often been the case; after all, in the Bible the widow is usually a symbol of poverty—with her dowry restored or not.

Divorce was slightly more complicated, though not particularly uncommon. And as you might imagine, men had more freedom to get out of marriages than women did—although "more freedom" is something of an understatement, since men could essentially divorce their wives for any reason, or no reason, at all. All the same, though it was not required, in most cases a man would, in fact, explain himself; Westbrook tells us that he might divorce his wife for "accumulating a private hoard, dissipating household resources and slandering her husband," all three of which, it could be said, might destabilize the household. You could also divorce your wife on moral grounds, says Westbrook, say, for "going out with her hair unbound, spinning in the street (which involved exposing herself[18]), speaking with strange men, or bathing where men bathe."

Technically, men were also allowed to marry more than one woman at a time. According to the Jewish scholar Adiel Schremer, "as long as polygyny did not threaten daily family life and was motivated by the wish to bear children (or any other positive motive)," apparently it was perfectly acceptable.[19]

---

18. Presumably too much of her arms or legs.

19. Schremer uses a word here—*polygyny*—that, when I first read it in an e-mail from a student helping me with this book, I figured was a typo, which is precisely

Acceptable, though, does not necessarily mean affordable, and even with two dowries, two wives would have been expensive to keep up. So men tended to have one wife (at a time).

And finally, although there's evidence that women did divorce their husbands in the first century, the exact circumstances that allowed for it are not clear. The New Testament, for example, records its happening, but doesn't offer much in terms of detail. A woman who divorces her husband and marries someone else is, according to Jesus, just as guilty of adultery as the husband who divorces his wife and marries someone else. (This is not, it should be noted, the typical Jewish line on second marriages.) Perhaps more common were situations in which a woman would, according to Henri Daniel-Rops,[20] "make herself so disagreeable that her husband would take the initiative." A woman might also get others—members of the religious authority, say—to lean on a husband to divorce her. This may have happened, according to Daniel-Rops, only "in a certain number of cases—duly established impotence; refusal

---

what I began to write in reply to the e-mail from my student. "Simon, Don't you mean *polygamy*?" But then I checked. Turns out I was wrong. Schremer explains, "The term usually applied to the phenomenon of one man being married to more than one woman simultaneously is 'polygamy.' This usage, however, is inaccurate; 'polygamy' refers to marriage with more than one spouse, be that of a man marrying more than one woman, or a woman marrying more than one man. The latter type of marriage is known from several societies, and termed 'polyandry[.]' . . . The precise term for the former is 'polygyny,'" which even my word processor doesn't recognize (Schremer, 181–82).

20. This, of course, is the same Daniel-Rops whom we've already established appeared, as late as 1962, to have some antiquated notions about the status of women in society. In this case, though, his description of the resourceful wife seems, at least to me, right on—if also a little stodgy.

to carry out matrimonial duties properly; habitual cruelty; a repulsive and incurable disease, such as leprosy; a change of trade and the adoption of a disgusting kind of work by the husband, such as the collection of dogs' dung[21] for tanners; or the decision to leave Palestine and live far away."

Ultimately, we see it once again—and once and for all: Palestine was home sweet home.

If we imagine the home as the inner workings of a family, the house tells the whole world who we are—or, looking back from our perspective, who we were—even if, when we look today, there's nothing left to see. Such is the case, for example, with Nazareth, where centuries of building projects (mainly churches) and millions of pilgrims and spiritual tourists have essentially wiped the remains of the first century from the face of the earth. It's not, we should say, entirely the fault of the Christians who have always seen Nazareth as one of the holiest sites in the world. Truth be told, when Nathanael of Cana took a swipe at Jesus and his hometown in John's Gospel, saying, "Can anything good come out of Nazareth?," he was only saying what everyone else around him was already thinking. Back then, Nazareth was a nothing town, of which there's almost nothing left.

---

21. Times appear to have changed in this regard. It's been decided in my home, for instance, that cleaning up after the dog is not only a respectable duty, but one that men are particularly well suited to.

Whatever roads existed in Nazareth were unpaved and there were no public buildings in town, just as there were no public inscriptions—another indication that almost no one there could read. Houses were built of stones and mud gathered from the fields and then topped with thatched reeds. Everything would have been one story. Your neighbor might have lived in a cave. The very few signs of life that archaeologists have been able to find from the first century include underground cisterns for water, some storage bins, stones for grinding grains into flour, vats to ferment and store wine, and pieces of locally made measuring cups and some other stone vessels. The fewer than 400 residents of Nazareth owned nothing of any value to anyone else and appear to have imported absolutely nothing from other parts of the world.

A slightly bigger place like Capernaum, the fishing village on the Sea of Galilee, with between 600 and 1,200 people, had only slightly more to say for itself than Nazareth, and from what we can tell, the rest of the world seemed to be paying it little attention.[22] No wealthy bureaucrat was having his named carved into a wall to announce his role as the town's benefactor—something that was typical in other, larger cities, like Caesarea Maritima. (Again, the number of people who could have read a public inscription like that would have been very small, anyway.)

What set Capernaum apart from Nazareth, though, apart

---

22. Well, to clarify: No one paid Capernaum any mind just so long as the taxes were paid on time.

from the fact that history has been kinder to the seaside town—
that is, history has left more for us to look at—was the arrangement and construction of houses you would have found there.
Even just slightly more people around allowed for greater coop-
eration—and probably larger, extended families, including, perhaps, the in-laws. Life here centered on a common courtyard,
with individual fieldstone apartments built up side by side on
foundations of large basalt boulders. Just like in Nazareth, the
stones making up the walls were rough and unhewn, held in
place with clay or mud or even animal dung, then smeared with
even more clay or mud or dung. As Reed tells us, they "were
constructed without the benefit of a skilled craftsman's techniques or tools."

The courtyard had a basic wooden door with a lock, which
was the only way into the complex, and individual apartments
offered only as much privacy as curtains or straw mats over the
doorways could provide—a fact that would probably weigh as
much in family planning as any worries you might have about
all those mouths to feed or dowries to pay. For what it's worth,
your windows were situated high, near what were exclusively
thatched roofs, allowing for light and ventilation but keeping
passersby from peering in on you asleep on another straw mat.
You would grind your flour, cook, and eat in the courtyard. As
in Nazareth, nearly all of your household items—storage jars,
grinding stones, looms, chalk vessels, oil lamps, and fishhooks,
say—were made locally. Your walls, inside and out, were plain,
without the plaster and frescos you might find in the home

of a Sepphorian landowner—not to say that you'd ever pay Sepphoris a visit.

Capernaum is presented a little more auspiciously in the
Gospels than Nazareth. That is, something good could have
come from there. Fish, for one thing. (Although maybe that's
about it.) But we're also told that Jesus and his followers spent
a lot of time there—unlike, say, in Nazareth or the capital city
of Sepphoris.[23] And though we've said from the beginning that
we wouldn't take much interest in stories about Jesus' travels
around Galilee, we are interested in the houses of the typical
Galileans he may have visited, and to a certain extent the ways
in which those houses were imagined back then.

When in the Gospel of Mark Jesus heals a paralytic in
Capernaum, in order to avoid the crowds that have gathered,
some men literally have to "unroof the roof" and lower the sick
man down to where Jesus is. This meant that they actually dug
through the reeds and packed mud of the roof.

---

23. There are a few theories about why Jesus might have avoided Sepphoris—it was
too Greek, some say; too rich, say others—but the one that seems most convinc-
ing to me has to do with what Jesus thought of Antipas. "That fox," as Jesus refers
to Antipas at one point, had killed John the Baptist, which would have given the
Baptist's onetime follower some reason for concern, especially since he had decided
to become a minister in his own right. A trip to Sepphoris at any point might have
been just as risky as that final trip to Jerusalem turned out to be. What's more, Reed
thinks that the reference to "that fox," plus the fact that Sepphoris's name in Hebrew,
Zippori, means "little bird," can actually help make some sense out of one of Jesus'
most confounding sayings: "Foxes have holes and birds of the sky have nests, but the
Son of man has nowhere to lay his head." In other words, this is a veiled reference to
the comfort and luxury of Antipas's Sepphoris, which stood in direct contrast to the
abject poverty of Jesus' countryside. The wealthy slept on alabaster headrests; Jesus
slept on a rock (Reed, 134–38).

This is not, as Reed and several others have pointed out, how Luke describes the scene in his version of the story. The essential plot points remain the same—Jesus heals the paralytic who, because of the crowds, had to be lowered into the house— but in Luke the man is lowered "through the tiles." Reeds vs. tiles: big difference.

It appears that Luke is guilty of something like what they call in the movies an "anachronism," or a continuity problem— say, for instance, in Sergio Leone's *Once Upon a Time in America*, where the 1970s NYC skyline appears across the East River from Prohibition-era Brooklyn. Such a mistake will rarely ruin a good story, but problems like this tend to be of great interest to film nerds. Likewise, these sorts of movie gaffes hardly ever tell us anything significant or meaningful about the moviemaker. They're forgiven almost as soon as we notice them, and they make us feel, at least for a moment, like we have something over on Sergio Leone.

The same cannot be said for biblical continuity problems, which get mined by Bible nerds for all they're worth. And what we might learn from Luke's account of going through a tile roof in Capernaum is not so much about the lone, exceptional tile-roofed house in a first-century Galilean village, where we already know houses were topped with thatched reeds and insulated with mud—something Mark confirms in his Gospel. Instead, it tells us something about Luke, who when writing the story for his audience would have done so in a way that would have made sense to them. What we can tell just from this little detail is that where Luke was writing—presumably a city, and some years after Mark—they almost certainly had tile roofs. And those tiles, like the reeds in Capernaum and Nazareth, would have said something about the people living there. Tiles meant civilized. Tiles meant Greek. Tiles meant money. The Christians that Luke knew sat under tile roofs. And to their minds so had Jesus.[24]

And yet still, whether your roof was made of tiles or made of reeds, or even if you lived in a cave, what we always have to remember is that in first-century Palestine the house your roof covered was a Jewish home. In fact, a detail we've already mentioned, although only in passing, is just as clear an indication of the people's ethnicity as the coins we saw in the last chapter and the complete lack of pig bones we'll see in the next: Everyone used limestone or chalk cups, mugs, bowls, and storage vessels—known to us as Herodian stoneware. These bowls and cups and huge jars were better than ceramic, because according to the Law, when reused, ceramics, as Crossan and Reed tell us, "impart impurity to later contents and also to their users."

---

24. As I've said before, one problem associated with talking about Jesus is that, almost without trying, we end up making claims about him that reveal how we understand him and reflect how we understand ourselves. What this example from the first century (or thereabouts) makes clear is that this has been happening ever since people first started talking and writing about him. And though it may be harmless, in this case the claim being made by Luke is that Jesus could sit under a tiled roof in a town that had no tiled roofs—not the kind of miracle Jesus would make his name on, but a miracle all the same.

Stone was from the earth and pure, "somewhat less a human product than a divine gift."[25]

If you were rich you had your huge chalk storage vessels turned on a lathe. If you were poor you made these items by hand, or maybe traded with a neighbor. They might have come with you as part of your dowry. But in the first century you kept them in your home so you could eat and drink.

And then, along with so many Jewish houses and homes in Palestine, by the second century those chalk vessels would virtually disappear.

---

25. Crossan and Reed go a little further explaining why stone was clean and materials like ceramics, or metal, or glass, which might have served the same purposes, were not. Apparently it's more of that local pride we saw in a previous chapter (and will, no doubt, see again): "[M]ost of the stone vessels have close parallels with glass, metal, and ceramic ones, which were imported and more expensive. Uncleanness was easily attributable to glass, metal, and ceramic vessels brought from the 'lands of the Gentiles,' that is to say imported luxury items. Stone was ritually pure, but it was also a cheap local product, a native material that could be made into vessels with relative ease" (Crossan and Reed, 165–68; Reed, 44, 45, 50, 51, 57, 127–28, 124, 160).

IV

FOOD IN YEAR ONE

Those who hunger and thirst for justice are blessed, since
they will feast.

—MATTHEW 5:6

And nobody pours young wine into old skins. If he does,
the wine will rip the skins, and then the wine is ruined
and the skins. Instead, pour young wine into fresh skins.

—MARK 2:21–22

Perhaps the most obvious thing to say about food in first-
century Palestine would be that the people did not eat pigs,
which to them was essentially how it had always been. The Law
had come down from God, through Moses himself, and was
first recorded in the Torah. More recently, in the mind of a first-
century peasant, this particular dietary law, along with circumcision, was at the heart of the revolution of the Hasmoneans,
who at first attacked the Seleucids with meat cleavers—which

seems appropriate—in defense of their (the Hasmoneans) refusal to sacrifice and eat pigs. It's worth bearing in mind, as well, just how important those Hasmonean heroes must have been to so many first-century Jews still collecting and exchanging their bronze coins. From Moses to the first rebel Mattathias and his son Judas (a.k.a. Maccabeus, "The Hammer"), God's people just did not eat pork. From an archaeological perspective, we know this today from what are called "bone profiles," which tell us what animal any given bone you dig out of the dirt comes from. Suffice it to say, the inhabitants of first-century Palestine didn't leave behind any pig bones.[1]

We could speculate about exactly what stands behind any Jewish dietary laws. Indeed, many have. And of all the Jewish laws about food, "NO PORK" might be both the best known and the most speculated about. In the case of pigs, cultural historians have tried to argue that by classifying these animals as "unclean," Jews avoid the health risk of trichinosis and other diseases.[2] Such

---

1. And this marks another of the unmistakable signposts leading us into life in first-century Palestine.

2. And yet, even today, the mere mention of pigs in Israel can be cause for alarm. In 2009, as the world braced itself against the spread of what quickly became known in the press as "swine flu," the Israeli Deputy Health Minister Yakov Litzman declared, "We will call it Mexico flu" (Associated Press, April 27, 2009), an accusation the Mexican ambassador to Beijing, Jorge Guajardo, would suggest was no better, reminding the press that it was a person, apparently from "Eurasia," who had brought the flu to Mexico in the first place. (Guajardo did not go so far as to rename it "Eurasia flu.") Not to be outdone, U.S. officials, under heavy pressure from pork producers and also hoping to dispel the myth that we were dealing with a food-borne illness, quickly took to calling it by its scientific name, the H1N1 virus (Bradsher, April 28, 2009). Of course, the end of the story is that to nearly everyone's dismay—except perhaps Mexico's—"swine flu" stuck (Cumming-Bruce and Jacobs, June 11, 2009).

explanations, of course, make Moses appear like a modern-day epidemiologist. And while hygiene and sanitation were of great concern to the people of this time in all areas of life—and really, going back as far as any of them could imagine—it's not an understanding of the dietary laws that we should assume for your typical, first-century Jew who thought about his food.[3] (And whether you thought all day about the Law, or spent all day working the fields, or hoarded grain and collected rents on a stall in the marketplace, everyone thought about his food.)

Even so, for us to call into question whether people who kept the Law knew the exact connection between pigs and parasitic roundworms is not to doubt the intelligence or even the powers of observation of anyone who lived in the first century.[4] And clearly, we can see what appears to be a similar concern with sanitation in the law against eating the carcasses of animals that have died of natural causes.[5] But that particular law concerning what is known biblically as *n'velah* contains a caveat that, if we look at other pieces of basic Jewish belief, should make us question whether dietary laws in general were initially, or, in the first century, concerned with sanitation and hygiene.

---

3. Nor should we assume that this is how anyone in the first century imagined Moses, who, it was believed, brought holiness, not an M.D. or Ph.D., down from Mount Sinai.

4. And as we'll see when I finally offer a diagnosis of exactly what killed King Herod, where powers of observation are concerned, I have to assume that first-century eyes were just as good as twenty-first-century ones—specifically, in fact, when it comes to identifying worms.

5. Deuteronomy 14:21, which concludes with the dietary law that keeps today's kosher-minded Jews from eating cheeseburgers: "You shall not boil a kid in its mother's milk."

First, the caveat. According to Deuteronomy, if you found a carcass you could "give it to aliens residing in your towns for them to eat, or you [could] sell it to a foreigner." And though he does take into consideration the nearly two thousand years of Jewish tradition that followed after what we're calling year one, the conclusion Rabbi David Feldman reaches about the law against n'velah makes pretty good sense and better measures the mind-set of a first-century Jew than for us to imagine anyone back then believing Moses was a modern-day M.D. specializing in preventative medicine. Feldman writes:

> Well, if Moses' intent were to prevent the spread of disease, he would never have permitted it [n'velah] to the "alien within thy gates." Clearly, the purpose is spiritual, to inculcate holiness by this discipline, as the verse itself insists.
>
> The point is sharper when this verse is compared with another: "There shall be one law, for you and for the alien in your midst" (Numbers 15:16). Both were to be equal before the civil law of the Torah, but these dietary provisions were "denominational," something for the Israelites alone.

Feldman reminds us here of Jewish distinctiveness—akin to what we elsewhere called a kind of "local pride." But what's even more important is the light he sheds on the problems Jews would have had breaking laws about showing concern for strangers (or faced with a rotten piece of meat, potentially killing someone with it). The dos and don'ts of Judaism could become a delicate balancing act, even in the times before rabbis began compiling their ongoing debate on the Law known to us today as the Talmud.[6] None of this is to say that health and hygiene were of no interest to first-century Jews where food laws were concerned; only, we shouldn't assume that preventing parasites was their main worry. After all, if the fear of disease (or even death) was keeping someone eating within the Law, it's easy to imagine that person taking a curious, albeit tentative, nibble.[7] Yet, if our zooarchaeological[8] evidence from the first century tells us anything, it's that the same cannot be said of the fear of God.

Knowing they were likely also blessed with a healthy dose of common sense against consuming anything that seemed to feed on trash or dead things, we have to assume that this same fear of God would have kept these people from eating other animals forbidden under kosher law. Beyond those we've already mentioned—pigs and animal carcasses—these included birds like vultures, sea

---

6. The New Testament offers us countless examples of this kind of first-century law debate. For example, we find Jesus answering questions about whether it's okay to pay the emperor his taxes and also making the claim that "the Sabbath exists for man, not man for the Sabbath" (Mark 2:27). In both cases, and in countless others, Jesus takes up a debatable point and offers his judgment, a ruling of sorts, a little like how judges today offer opinions on a law's constitutionality. And now, what I'll insist again is that whether you believe Jesus ever said these things about the Sabbath, or taxes, or both, neither adds nor takes away from the fact that people in the first century would have understood this argumentative approach to the Law. And it's something that we recognize today, as well.

7. People take those kinds of risks all the time, often when food is scarce—say, on CBS's hit TV series *Survivor* or the Discovery Channel's *Survivorman*—or seen as an exotic luxury, like in a plate of *fugu*, dramatically eaten by celebrity chef Anthony Bourdain. "Fugu. The deadly puffer fish of legend. It's a delicacy. It's expensive. . . . It can kill you" (Bourdain, 153).

8. The kind of archaeology related to animal remains, which is where we get the bone profiles.

gulls, ravens, and hawks, among several others named specifically in the Torah[9] (including, oddly, bats, which, of course, aren't birds at all) and also animals that "swarm on the ground," like rodents, lizards, and most insects.[10] Animals you could eat included those with cloven hoofs that also chew their cud—which allows cows but, again, prohibits pigs—and any fish with scales and fins.[11] As for plants and fruits, anything goes—unlike in Eden, where the fruits of one particular tree were off-limits.

So what we've established so far is a pretty good baseline for understanding the diet of people living in first-century Palestine. Beginning with hard evidence that no one was eating pigs, we can somewhat safely figure that they weren't eating other unclean foods either. And beginning there, we can simply say that what people ate in the first century constituted a fairly typical agrarian diet of the Mediterranean—one that we would surely recognize today. They ate olives and olive oil, figs, dates, pomegranates, legumes, cheese, and different butters (churned at home), on rare occasion some small amount of beef, veal, lamb, or mutton, fish, if you lived near the coasts, and small roasted fowls. Cow or goat milk would have been drunk fresh

---

9. Deuteronomy 14:12–18, which basically prohibits carrion eaters and birds of prey.

10. Locusts, of course, being the most famous exception, which, according to Oded Borowski, would have been "grilled on skewers or fried" (Borowski, 72). And although it's debated whether the proper translation of the Greek word *akris* is "locust" (the bug) or "locust" (the tree), of which someone would have presumably eaten the pods, I agree with most scholars that John the Baptist—by all accounts an early Survivorman—ate insects and honey (honey that, of course, was clean, but which came from bees that, by Law, were not) (Leviticus 11:20–23; Mark 1:6; Matthew 3:4).

11. Which would exclude, just for example, Bourdain's *fugu*.

or processed into yogurt (also a drink), which would have given them whey, which they would have likewise consumed.

Since fermentation was the best way to preserve grape juice (or even the juice of pomegranates or dates), wine was ubiquitous; then as now, drinking was a good way to end a long, hard day in the vineyards. And biblical scholar Oded Borowski has suggested that beer was a fairly common drink in Palestine, mainly on account of where it was: "Since Egypt and Mesopotamia were well known as beer producers, it can be safely assumed that beer was also known in Israel, which is located between the two." There were some vegetables—onions, garlic, and dandelion greens, to name a few—as well as nuts, other wild greens, and berries that we know were eaten by the people of the Land.

Ultimately, just as today, in the first century there was a wide variety of foods available. But that said, you could count on every meal to begin with some bread, and bread would have made up some 70 percent of the calories a person would have consumed in a given day. (On average, a Galilean would have consumed about 550 pounds of grain each year.) It should come as no surprise that the same word used for bread, *lehem*, was used for food in general. And rather than using plates, most of what was served—from olives to lentils to that rare piece of meat or fish—was scooped out or laid across a piece of pita. In other words, the entire first-century diet—and in ways, much, much more than that—rested on what you could make from those fields of grain.

Translators of Josephus call this grain "corn," which shouldn't be confused with the corn we're familiar with in United States, *zea mays*, native to Central America and unknown to the rest of the world until 1492.[12] What they had was barley (i.e., barleycorn) and wheat, planted between November and January, and then harvested in April and May—barley first, then wheat. They also would have grown some oats, along with millet and the reaching purple grain known as lupine, or the bitter termis bean, as well; although not a normal part of the diet, these last two grains were sturdy and kept well and could be eaten in a pinch. (Today, lupine, which I've seen growing wild along the highways of New England in early summer, is mainly used as animal feed.)

Under what had been normal conditions—that is, before Galilee's population explosion under Herod Antipas—typical farming families would have strived for self-sufficiency, with neighbors working together in order to sustain the small populations of small villages. They would have eaten together, either in the courtyard or in a large room in one of the apartments, depending on the season. This is what we would have seen in Nazareth, or even in a fishing community like Capernaum on the Sea of Galilee, only there we would expect more fish—a lot of it dried. The land in Capernaum was considerably less fertile than what you could find to the west, in what's known as the Gennesar Plain.[13] In general, though, villagers would have

---

12. Although we'll see that the corn of Josephus's day was, in a way, not so different from the corn of today—and I'm not talking here about the way it tasted, but the way it's been used, and, strange though it is to say, the way it's used us.

13. In what we might consider today a fine bit of nature writing, which he managed to wedge into an account of the Roman assault on Galilee in 67 CE, Josephus marvels

grown a variety of crops in a variety of small fields, regularly leaving whole pieces of farmable land unsown during a given season, which benefitted the land itself and protected against crop failure.[14]

The grain harvest began with the Festival of Unleavened Bread, or Passover, and ended with the Festival of Pentecost, which in the book of Exodus is also called the Feast of Harvest. Grains were then gathered and stored in small barns, underground silos, and caves. Families would have traded or shared from their surplus with neighbors. And we can further imagine these peasant families gathering smaller amounts from the larger stores and then grinding their own grain into flour using a large stone and a small stone. They would mix the flour with water, and after kneading it into dough, they would then bake rounds of bread against the wall of a wood- or charcoal-burning oven situated in the courtyard between their homes. Using the flour they stored in stone jars, families would make bread every day. The harvest would last until the following year's harvest.

---

over the fertility and natural diversity of the Gennesar Plain, which sounds to me a little like the vegetarian version of the lion lying down with the lamb:

> Thanks to the rich soil there is not a plant that does not flourish there, and the inhabitants grow everything: the air is so temperate that it suits the most diverse species. Walnuts, most winter-loving of trees, flourish in abundance, as do palms, which thrive on heat, side by side with figs and olives, for which a milder air is indicated. (Josephus, *The Jewish War*, 231)

14. The Law itself required fields to be left fallow every seven years—the Sabbatical year—although there's no way of knowing whether the Law was always, or ever, dutifully adhered to in this case, or whether, after the agricultural needs of Galilee exploded during Antipas's reign, Jewish peasants would have even been allowed to leave the land unplanted.

It's likely this description oversimplifies this situation some-what. But even if we bear in mind how hard it would have been to work mainly by hand day in and day out, where food was concerned, life itself in Galilee was fairly simple.

Or, things were fairly simple until, all of a sudden, with Antipas, they just weren't anymore.

As we know, things became much more complicated for Galilean farmers after Antipas built the cities of Sepphoris and Tiberias. The surrounding rural areas were almost entirely sold off for tax money and bought up by wealthy city-dwellers who developed the land they'd invested in within an inch of its life—hiring the former landowners to sow one new field after another, tearing up the ground and blanketing the land with crops.

To a certain extent, this is ground we've already covered. And yet, what's important to understand is that as fields and orchards and vineyards grew and grew into massive estates, and areas of the countryside that had been previously unfarmed were terraced for trees and vines, many rural communities lost control over the production of not just wine and olive oil, but also over the processing of the basis of their entire diet: grain.

Most production and storage of grain became centralized, taking place inside and immediately surrounding the cities. In times of need—say during a crop failure, famine, or drought—farmers began having to buy the very crops they had planted and harvested, threshed and ground into flour, even as the new money flowing through Galilee allowed for new landowners to yoke oxen and plow under even more land to grow even more grain. Forced to abandon their traditional farming practices, inhabitants of the Holy Land—or once again, more simply, the Land—looked on as Palestine's essential richness was all but stripped away. After all, as we know today—and as they would have witnessed in the first century—growing a single crop on a given piece of land year after year disrupts natural biodiversity and the long-term productivity of the soil. For instance, the overcultivation of certain olive trees would have resulted in the loss of some varieties that grew wild. Growing grain, and only grain, drained the land of its nutrients.

Indeed, it's hardly going too far to call these years at the start of the first century the birth of big agribusiness.[15] It might be said, in fact, that during the first century a displaced tenant farmer in Galilee was witness to an ancient version of what food writer Michael Pollan, author of *The Omnivore's Dilemma*, has described in America as the "Conquest of Corn." And in those terms, we might call the dilemma facing the first-century peasant in Palestine the "Conquest of Barleycorn."[16]

Under the rule of Antipas, this single grain began to look

---

15. What today we call Cargill and Monsanto and Perdue was, in the first century, known by the brand name Antipas. Or a bigger brand name still—*Caesar*.

16. Pollan's larger story—about how corn weaseled its way into more than a full quarter of the 45,000 products found in your average supermarket—is, in some ways, about the technology available today that allows us to turn a highly versatile grass into everything from toothpaste to Twinkies, disposable diapers to fiberglass, and matches to pesticides (Pollan, 17, 19), none of which had a place in daily life of the first century. Still, despite their inability during the first century to process Josephus's "corn" into some form of commercial cosmetics or high-fructose barleycorn syrup, looking back, the impulse driving first-century agriculture—that is, the commercial requirements of Empire—feels eerily familiar today.

like what Pollan describes as the "protocapitalist plant," developing the very same "dual identity" of today's *zea mays*: It was both food and commodity. Technically, the shift that occurred under the massive economic and population pressures of first-century Galilee was a move from traditional polycropping to commercial monocropping. In other words, what had been self-sustaining farms, growing all the variety of foods a family needed, were all but consumed by the cultivation of a single crop that could not possibly sustain them no matter how much of it they produced.

And if the first century lacked its James Agee to create a record of the poorest of the poor, it just as certainly lacked its Michael Pollan to look carefully at the intimate relationship between people and the food they grow. Yet, if you listen carefully to what Pollan says about the ways in which corn has taken over fields of America—today covering some 80 million acres of the country—sometimes you'd swear he was talking about what happened to Galilee as it attempted to feed the growing populations of its wealthy cities, almost always at the expense of not just the rural peasants but also the farmland they plowed. Remember, just 3 percent of Galilee's arable land was left undeveloped under Herod Antipas.[17]

To the displaced peasants we've been most concerned with, or even those who looked on as their neighbors were moved

---

17. By comparison, Pollan tells us this about Iowa today: "A mere 2 percent of the state's land remains what it used to be (tall-grass prairie), every square foot of the rest having been completely remade by man" (Pollan, 38).

off the land, the sudden shift away from tending small fields for you and your family would have been as much a religious problem as an ecological, agricultural, or economic one. Indeed, there's a certain kind of nostalgia about agriculture in the Bible, where it's remembered that farmers "tilled their land in peace" and "the ground gave its increase." One hears a wistfulness in these recollections from 1 Maccabees, where "old men sat in the streets; they all talked together of good things." And God was known to be responsible for all good things.

At this point it may simply be better if we come to terms with the idea that it's only from our perspective today that religion, ecology, agriculture, and economics can be understood as discrete categories at all. After all, in year one it was believed that God watched over every coin that changed hands, every seed planted, every tree uprooted, every animal roasted, and every parcel of his land left fallow. Because once again, it was all God's—both the land and its people. And God had laws concerning the things that belonged to him—for instance, the one we've already mentioned that allowed the fields their rest every seven years, just as people rested every seventh day.

J. D. Crossan and Jonathan Reed have identified two specific pieces of scripture that were meant to shape the intimate first-century relationship—if not also the eternal one—between the people and the land, which in turn was supposed to establish the right relationship between those people and the food they grew on that land. In Leviticus, for instance, God announces that "the land shall not be sold in perpetuity, for the land is mine; with me you are but aliens and tenants." What's more, Crossan and Reed point out, the prophet Isaiah curses those "who join house to house, who add field to field, until there is room for no one but you, and you are left to live alone in the midst of the land!" Most essentially, the authors conclude, the problem the prophets "inveigh[ed] against [was] the inevitable human drive for fewer and fewer people to have more and more land and for more and more people to have less and less land." Within God's kingdom—where God himself was just—the unprecedented development of the land and displacement of the people that took place in Roman Palestine was supposed to be impossible. Elsewhere in the Scripture we're reminded again that the land is God's, and in God's kingdom, debts are supposed to be forgiven, charging interest is forbidden, and as Leviticus makes clear to all the people—especially the displaced and dispossessed, the tenant farmer and the slave—no matter how bad things had gotten, every fifty years you could count on the land to return to the way it once was: "You shall hallow the fiftieth year and you shall proclaim liberty throughout the land to all its inhabitants. It shall be a jubilee for you: you shall return, every one of you, to your property and every one of you to your family." And yet, the impossible seems to have happened. God's kingdom was taken away from God and his people. There's simply no evidence that this part of the Law, or the warning from the prophet Isaiah, meant much among wealthy landowners—who ate just as little pork and used the same kind of stone jars as the peasants they hired to grow their grain.

It's a strange conclusion to reach. By some measures, everyone was Jewish. And being distinctively Jewish mattered. Yet, what made the laws against joining house to house and field to field less important to a wealthy landowner than dietary laws against eating pork is anybody's guess. But my sense is that in Roman Palestine, within one generation, it was becoming clear to an increasing number of people that grain, and not God, was king. And like corn in the United States today, grain in Palestine, which had always been simply a part of the history of the eternal kingdom of God in all its variety, was now, like nearly everything else, a piece of the Empire—the growing kingdom of man.

V

BATHS IN YEAR ONE

And for you, even the hairs on your head—every one of them—have been counted up.

—MATTHEW 10:30

I t should come as no surprise by now that people in the first century would have had to deal with lots and lots of filth. Filth of every kind imaginable. We've already seen that a woman might try to convince her husband to divorce her if, day in, day out, he came home stinking to high heaven after collecting dung for leather tanners—and bear in mind, this would have come from a woman whose walls were themselves plastered with dung and whose floors were, essentially, nothing but packed dirt. We've also heard a little about the most devout of all Jewish groups of the time, the Essenes, who, it turns out, had their own issues with dung. They lived in a wilderness compound call Qumran and rigidly kept the Sabbath—that is, did not work from sundown Friday to sundown Saturday. By Josephus's account, what this meant is that on the Sabbath the Essenes did not even "go to ease themselves."[1] On other days, though, the Essenes, equipped with one tool and one tool only—a hatchet—would find "the more secluded spots" outside Qumran, cloak themselves "so as not to affront the rays of God," and defacate in a hole they would dig themselves. "Then," says Josephus, "they put the excavated soil back in the hole."[2] In other words, it wasn't just the filth of animals that offended first-century sensibilities. Then as now, people even disgusted themselves.

A major city like Jerusalem, apart from its ancient system of running water, had what was called the Dung Gate, which led out into what was known as Gehenna—hell itself—where the city's waste, trash, and even its dead animals were burned in what must have seemed like a perpetual fire. A smaller city

---

1. The Essenes were the group of pious men we heard about earlier who, according to Josephus, were "afraid of the promiscuity of women and convinced that none of the sex remain[ed] faithful to one man" (Josephus, *The Jewish War*, 133, 135–36). Not to put too fine a point on it, but they were also, it seems, ritually anal-retentive.

2. To be fair, the Bible does actually stipulate just this sort of six-day-per-week, one-time-use, personal privy for encamped soldiers holding ground against an enemy. That the Essenes also took care of business this way says a lot about how they saw themselves in relation to a whole world of other Jews living in the cities and countryside of Palestine, and carrying on as best they could under the Empire. Basically, the Essenes relieved themselves like soldiers because they thought of themselves as soldiers. And they were fighting against the whole world. (Presumably, of course, the Essenes would also have followed the directives concerning nocturnal emissions that immediately precede the biblical instructions for relieving yourself: "If one of you becomes unclean because of a nocturnal emission, then he shall go outside the camp; he must not come within the camp. When evening comes, he shall wash himself with water, and when the sun has set, he may come back into the camp" [Deuteronomy 23:10–11].)

like Sepphoris had what archaeologists identify today as a sewage system, which ran under the paving stones covering the wide *cardo*, durable enough "to survive five hundred years of wagon wheels that cut ruts into the street." What that tells us is that city planners had sewage on their minds, and that in Sepphoris they used the sturdiest materials available to keep it out of sight, or at the very least, out of the sight of shoppers. With the smell, though, it's doubtful whether out of sight would have always meant out of mind (indeed, it would clearly not have been *out of scent*). And we can assume that even with a regular flow of runoff from the winter rains, one would have tried to avoid spending too much time at the far end of Sepphoris's Main Street, where property values and rents on storefronts must have dropped off precipitously.

Capernaum, on the other hand, that very modest fishing town, had no sewage system at all, and waste of any kind—sweepings, ashes, wastewater, whatever—would have been collected by families and poured out into the alleyways between the houses. With streets of packed dirt—dusty in the dry months, muddy in the rain—who could tell the difference between what was there to begin with and what had accumulated over years of waste disposal unaided by any inner public workings? It's no wonder that during construction homebuilders situated their windows as far from the ground as possible. Still, even that wouldn't have been enough to keep out the stench. Given their best efforts against what must have been really foul-smelling passages around town, over time all that rubbish and refuse would pile up—in effect, raising street level, or lowering the houses, depending on your view—and leave those windows no longer quite so far out of reach.

What a town like Capernaum had over a smaller inland village like Nazareth, though, was its proximity to a body of water. People who lived near a river or lake or even a brook—most obviously the Jordan River or the Sea of Galilee—were able to keep themselves cleaner than a villager in a place without easy access to fresh water. (Nazareth's main and meager water source, now known as the Well of Mary, trickled along its western edge.) With their inhabitants relying more on fish, seaside towns might also have had to keep fewer farm animals, which would have meant less animal dung to dispose of. This might have something to do with why a place like Nazareth, without much of local body of water to speak of and relying for the most part on wells, would have remained so small. A town can only take so much concentrated stink. Consequently, we could expect that, as much as possible, farmers throughout Palestine would have gathered manure and spread it on their fields, putting some of that stink to good use. Indeed, in the rare and direst situations, historically Jews were also believed to have used human dung for the same purpose. In the book of Ezekiel, it's even imagined as a fuel to bake bread.[3]

---

3. This particular use of human filth was to come down as the punishment of an angry God against an unfaithful Jerusalem, and it makes the prophet Ezekiel buck a little. He complains, "Ah Lord God! I have never defiled myself." To which God replies, apparently trying to comfort Ezekiel, "See, I will let you have cow's dung instead of human dung, on which you may prepare your bread" (Ezekiel 4:12–15). This would surely have been of some comfort—but seriously, what does God mean here by "on which"?

What's more, with fishing the main occupation in Capernaum, inhabitants may have spent somewhat less time in the fields than a Nazarene, whose life was almost exclusively agricultural. This means that someone in Capernaum, who kept his hands out of the dirt, might simply have kept himself a little cleaner in general.

Still, it's safe to say that fishermen can accumulate their very own kind of filth. And given what we've seen of options available to the wife of a dung collector, you can easily imagine the wife of a fisherman requesting her husband go jump in a lake every day after work. After a day spent with her children and endless housekeeping—salting, drying, and grilling fish; sweeping up; making bread; pressing olives; squeezing grapes; and on and on—it's also not difficult to picture that wife, every once in a while, finding a place among other women[4] for an evening dip as well. And given the separation of the sexes, there's also no need to think that first-century swimmers spent much time thinking about bathing suits.

The bottom line, though, was this: Hard as they tried to keep the filth away from them, anything that we would recognize as proper sanitation would have been impossible in the first century, especially among peasants. Adding to the well water, which itself was used mainly for drinking and for baking (as a main ingredient of bread), rain would have been of only modest value in terms of keeping things physically clean, especially

---

4. Unless, of course, she wanted to be sent packing. Remember, of course, a husband could divorce his wife if she were caught "bathing where men bathe" (Westbrook, 155).

since most of what was collected would have been diverted from the streets, courtyards, or animal pens, where families would have kept their stinking goats or cows and also done most of their washing. Rainwater was collected and poured into plastered bathtubs. And in a tiny place like Nazareth, filling one or two of these public baths with water was more important to the people than keeping their homes and animal pens spic-and-span. Fortunately, it was also more feasible.

Now, with this first mention of first-century baths, we should stop and make an important point about cleanliness in year one. Back then you could be two different kinds of dirty. Which also meant that you could be two different kinds of clean. They were, in some cases, related, and as it happens, water was important to making yourself both sorts of clean. The main difference is that while one kind of cleaning made you simply cleaner, the other sort of cleaning made you both cleaner and distinctly Jewish.

The first sort of cleanliness is perhaps more familiar to us, and today involves things like washing our face and hair, scrubbing our backs and behind our ears (or for the more obsessive among us, using instant hand sanitizer before, during, and after a ride on public transportation). And in general, we're talking about not just being physically clean, but seeming that way, too—both to ourselves and to others. This sort of cleanliness is the type we can afford today because it's cheap, convenient, and fairly simple.

In the first century, keeping physically clean was rarely as simple or as common as we know it to be today. Nowadays, anywhere there is a faucet, a shower, a washing machine, a dish-washer, even a bidet—plus maybe the odd bit of soap—we have a chance to wash. And just think of this: Both public swimming pools and public beaches typically have showers, which means that we're so clean today that we wash ourselves both before we wash ourselves and after we wash ourselves. Now think of someone sweeping her dirt floors, sleeping under a roof insulated with flaking mud, and at the end of the day sitting against a wall plastered with cow dung, and you should get a sense of just how unconcerned with physical filth a typical first-century peasant would have allowed herself to be.

This is not to say that people weren't trying to be clean. Sweeping a dirt floor is still sweeping. A dip in the Sea of Galilee is still a dip in the sea. And wheeling your trash out of the city to burn it is not so different from some of our own waste-disposal solutions.[5] It's not too much to think that people at least tried to keep their hands and faces basically clean, and as we see throughout both the Hebrew Bible and the New Testament, possibly their feet as well. Rules of hospitality recommended you offer your guests the chance to remove their sandals and wash in a large stone bowl or pot when they arrived at your door.[6]

---

5. What's more, people in the first century knew that a growing mound of trash that burned for what must have seemed like eternity was the very picture of hell—essentially, a hell on earth. It's a lesson we've heard over and over in the movies. From *Soylent Green* and *Blade Runner* to *An Inconvenient Truth* and WALL-E we've been asked time and again, *What to do with all this stuff!?* And indeed, if any question is an eternal one, this seems to be it.

6. Some scholars go further to include not just foot washing as part of the typical measures taken for hospitality's sake, but also some oil to anoint the head, and a kiss (Meeks et al., 1972). We can assume people in the first century would have done these things with more or less consistency and enthusiasm. That said, offering someone the chance to wash his feet would have had a similar effect as asking a guest nowadays to leave his shoes at the door, which we all know benefits the host at least as much as the

Now, in general, at least according to the biblical scholar Oded Borowski, women would have been more diligent than men about cleanliness—"most likely," he surmises, "as part of flirting."[7] And to cover up body odor everyone would have used perfumes[8]— the same substances used to cover up the stink of the dead. In general, peasant men would have tried to keep their hair short to avoid having to keep it clean—although just as we see among the most observant Jews today, the locks at their temples would probably have grown long. Beards, we might safely assume, were also kept trimmed as much as possible.[9] Women, in general, would have let their hair grow long, but kept it covered. Houses were kept smelling fresh with incense and spices, although you might imagine the smell of olive oil would have dominated everything. It burned in flat clay lamps with a wick sticking out one end,

guest, and sends some of us scrambling to find a pair of un-holey socks the morning before a visit to so-and-so's house.

7.   You may have noticed this before, but regardless of whatever anecdotal evidence Borowski may provide from the Song of Songs, the book of Ruth, or the *Anchor Bible Dictionary*, I think it's best if we take his speculations into the sex lives of first-century women, be they flirting daughters or working prostitutes, always with a grain of salt.

8.   Although again Borowski supposes that women would have been more generous with perfumes than men.

9.   Of course now we're getting into decisions that today are matters of taste, I suppose, and to say more in general about how anyone kept his hair or beard would be to assume that the man had no preferences or choice in the first century. If we can speculate that women used perfume to go flirting, we might as well assume that men, too, could make individual choices about grooming that mattered both to them and to the people around them. And not, I hope, to make too much of comparisons with modern tenant farmers, we find that, tattered as his clothes may appear in Walker Evans's photographs for *Let Us Now Praise Famous Men*, Bud Fields still wears a proud and dignified salt-and-pepper mustache. And for that matter, writing about the clothes of another Southern peasant, Floyd Burroughs, James Agee notes: "The crease is still sharp in the trousers" (Agee and Evans, 257).

giving off a dim light, and was situated in a hole in the wall or up at the top of a stand. It would have burned all day and all night.

In the end, though, there's little hard evidence that anyone used much soap. If and when they did, it likely would have been soft potash soap made from the lye that came from wood ashes. (These people were nothing if not resourceful, making soap out of dust.) They would have used the same stuff to clean their clothes, and as we might figure, the wealthy would probably have done laundry, and washed in general, more frequently. Professional launderers—simply out of reach for most people— would have had spots near sources of water where they carried out their jobs. Soap cost extra.

These facts are good for us to know, because they get us to our second kind of dirty and, even better, our second kind of clean—a cleanliness, in fact, that had nothing at all to do with soap. The prophet Jeremiah had been clear about that:

> Though you wash yourself with lye
> and use much soap,
> the stain of your guilt is still before me,
> says the Lord God.

All a jeremiad like this goes to show is that cleanliness was just one more part of your life that God has something to say about.[10] And what he said is that soap couldn't handle the kind

---

10. Of course, one could rightly ask what part of life God didn't have something to say about.

of stain that most offended him. In first-century Palestine—
again from Judea in the south to Galilee in the north—what
was clear to everyone, and indeed, what once again set you
apart, was your obsession with being ritually pure.

Some of this we've already seen. For instance, we've already
mentioned the limestone and chalk used to make reusable cups
and bowls and basins. The material would have been considered
perpetually pure, and using it would have left you pure, as well.
The same can't be said for a ceramic cup that was used more
than once, or a glass bottle, or a metal bowl. They would have
been rejected as impure after one use. Likewise, when it came
to food, certain animals—particularly pigs—would have left an
equally dark stain. In all these cases, washing your mouth out
with soap would have been no remedy at all.[11]

But the people's concern for purity was far more comprehensive than any set of dietary laws could take complete account
of.[12] Purity and impurity were measured on a scale that cov-

---

11. Good thing, too. The soap in those days could have killed you.

12. We've heard it already from Jesus: "What goes into the mouth does not corrupt
a man, but what comes from the mouth, this corrupts a man" (Matthew 15:11). And
while this has often been taken to mean that Jesus stood against Jewish dietary laws, I
think it's possible to take it to mean that, for him, purity was much more complicated
and thoroughly comprehensive than a system of dos and don'ts when it came to food,
and that avoiding pork meant no less to God than speaking out justly and truth-
fully, just for example. Now, when we say that, in Jesus' mind, avoiding pork probably
meant no less to God than justice and truth, we shouldn't jump to the conclusion
that Jesus thought avoiding pork meant no more to God than those things, either;
after all, when we consider what archaeologists were able to discover throughout first-
century Palestine, we see that Jesus and his friends and followers don't seem to have
left behind any more, or any less, pork than anyone else did—that is, nobody left
anything behind.

ered the whole world. For now, though, let's look at an isolated example, with the hope of seeing through first-century eyes the difference between being physically clean and ritually pure.

Our example is from the Book of Tobit. Though it is apocryphal—that is, not officially part of the Jewish Scriptures—and also written hundreds of years before the first century, in a culture where stories are often passed down by word of mouth, Tobit's tale was part of Jewish folklore.[13] In the first century, his would have been a household name. And in his story, we see some real life played out before us—nothing super heroic, no apocalypse, no prophecies, no belly of any whale. In specific, people in the first century would have found the same thing we do in the book: a story of ritual purity in the face of a corpse—or rather, in the face of someone, Tobit, who touches a corpse.

The scenario goes like this: Tobit is about to enjoy a good dinner with his wife Anna and his son Tobias during the festival of Pentecost, or, as we've already heard it called, the Feast of Harvest. Before they begin, however, Tobit sends his son out to invite "whatever poor person you may find of our people"—that is, another Jew—"and he shall eat together with me."[14] Hospitality is virtue. Well, Tobias does his father one better, finding not a poor person, but a dead, strangled person *of their*

---

13. Not to confuse matters, but the Book of Tobit is widely understood to be fictional, which calling it folklore might imply; J. D. Crossan goes so far as to call it a novel (Crossan, *The Birth of Christianity*, 553), a genre of fiction that most scholars of literature would say didn't actually exist until the eighteenth century, arguably with the publication of *Robinson Crusoe* in 1719.

14. Just as we might expect, Tobit's "with me"—in other words, not "with us"—shows him as a typically self-important *oikodespotes*.

people,[15] "murdered and thrown into the marketplace." Hearing this, and before taking even a bite of his dinner the story seems proud to note, Tobit dashes off to collect the man from the marketplace and then deposits the body in one of his rooms, where it would have to rest until sundown, when he could bury it. It's here where things go badly for poor Tobit—and all for the sake of purity.

Touching a corpse would have made Tobit impure, a detail of the story that would have struck someone in the first century as much in Tobit's own time. And knowing this, he washes himself after putting the body away and then returns to what was a very emotional, mournful dinner. "And I wept," he says. After sunset, Tobit goes off to dig a grave and buries the body. He washes again—presumably scrubbing himself clean of both kinds of filth—and then, rather than going into the house to sleep with his wife, Tobit curls up against the wall in his courtyard. For purity reasons, the house itself was off-limits.[16] And for her part, Tobit's wife Anna, we can presume, would have preferred to remain ritually clean herself.

It was hot in the courtyard that night, and Tobit drifted off to sleep without covering his face. This was a mistake. Throughout

---

15. All this emphasis on one Jew helping another Jews tells us two things: first, that Tobit lived in a society where Jews lived among non-Jews—that is, in exile from the Holy Land—and second, that there is something not just less pressing about helping a non-Jew, but also, as we'll see, doing so could actually defile you.

16. Some scholars have wondered what made it okay for Tobit to eat dinner in his house but not okay for him to sleep there (Meeks et al., 1441). To me the answer seems fairly obvious: The family wouldn't have been eating in the house at all, but rather in the breezy comfort of their courtyard.

the night, the story goes, sparrows walked along the top of the courtyard wall, and as they're known to do, eased themselves over the side, right into Tobit's eyes. This produced what Tobit calls "white films," which were only made worse when physicians treated him with ointments. The Law seems not to have required him to wash his eyes, however, and nowhere in the story does he try splashing some water on his face, not even when he wakes up unable to see straight.

In other words, Tobit's story would have told someone in the first century that it was more offensive to touch a dead body—even a freshly strangled one—than to have your face covered in bird droppings. And such a lesson would have made its own kind of sense. In a world where normal, everyday filth was just that—normal and everyday—keeping yourself ritually pure must have seemed, in its own way, a lot easier. And if you believed the folklore, what seemed to matter most was how pure you were and how conscientious you were when you encountered something that wasn't. Holiness itself would have been seen as a measure not of piety but of purity. And Tobit had actually conducted himself in ways that would have kept him in God's good graces. This would have been excellent news to peasants whose streets were literally made out of trash and who washed themselves with soap maybe once a month—if ever. After all, if everyone went around stinking to high heaven—or worse, to my mind, getting defecated on by a bunch of nasty sparrows—what could have set you apart from your neighbor was how, and how well, you kept yourself ritually clean.

Menstruating women were unclean. Anyone who touched a menstruating woman was unclean. Anyone who touched a corpse was unclean. Anyone who touched someone who had touched a corpse was unclean. If you had a nocturnal emission you were unclean. Anyone who touched anyone who had had a nocturnal emission was unclean. Foreigners were unclean, and contact with them threatened you, too. And so on. You get the idea. Basically, at some point, everyone—women more than men, it would seem—became ritually unclean. In a sense, both life itself and the Law seemed to require it. After all, women have to menstruate if you want them to have children; Tobit was being a total *mensch* when he buried the dead guy from the marketplace. And yet, since the Law insisted on purity, the people needed a place to clean themselves.

Nowhere was this insistence on purity more obvious than in Jerusalem itself. There, archaeologists have found hundreds of the first-century ritual baths known *miqwaoth*. And if the number of baths—both public and private—tells us anything, it's that for anyone living in the city, or for the thousands of pilgrims that showed up every year for religious festivals, it would have been fairly simple to keep yourself ritually clean in the city of the house of God. During the festivals we can imagine there were probably lines, especially around the entrances to the Temple Mount, the furthest reaches of the Temple complex itself, where these public baths were most common.

Cleanliness was, in this case, literally next to godliness.

Which was a good thing: You couldn't get into the Temple unless you were considered ritually pure. And the *miqwaoth* would have done the trick. Using a public pool by the Temple would have been like a Catholic today taking a dip in a massive pool of holy water at the entrance to his church, rather than simply touching his index finger to the little bowl of holy water at the door, before strolling in.

It might begin to seem like we're splitting hairs, but as you might expect, even the Temple itself had a whole system of purity concerns—limits, you might call them—even after you'd moved beyond the pools at the entrance. People would have thought of it this way, beginning—and again, as you might expect—with the Holy Land itself: The whole rest of the world is profane next to the Holy Land; the Land is profane next to the Temple Mount; the Temple Mount is profane next to the Temple itself, and so on, through a whole series of courtyards—the Court of the Gentiles, the Women, the Israelites, the Priests, etc. And who you were determined how far you could go toward the purest place in the universe. At the center of the Temple was what's known as "the throne place," imagined to be "the place of the soles of [God's] feet"[17]—the Holy of Holies. And only the High Priest, holiest and purest of all men,[18] would have been allowed inside the Holy of Holies, and him only twice a year.

---

17. God wore exactly a size 20 cubits, extra wide (Ezekiel 41:4).

18. Again, of course, *men*. Any women would have been left behind several courtyards back, in the Court of Women, which meant they were purer than any non-Jew, but by no means as pure as any Jewish man.

Away from the Temple, a typical private bath around Jerusalem or out in the countryside surrounding the city had a double entrance and steps with a low partition leading down to two adjacent pools connected with a pipe or channel. You likely moved through the bath from one side to another, ritually cleaning yourself along the way. What's peculiar about the baths archaeologists have found in the areas around Jerusalem is that a great many of them were built alongside agricultural installations like olive and wine presses, as if planned as part of the installations themselves. Because so much of what was grown in the countryside was presumably used in the Temple during rituals, the wine and olive oil producers of Judea had to be ritually pure at all times, it seems. As we've said, impurity was seen to be contagious—like a food-borne illness, in this case, even in food that was, in and of itself, pure. And in order to move up the hierarchy of purity—and I mean *literally up*, from the Land to the Mount, and then to the Temple itself and through all those courtyards of increasing holiness—the food itself had to begin pure and stay pure the whole way. Grapes were stomped by clean feet. Olives ground by pure hands. And yet there's no reason to think that anyone at the bath would have touched even a lick of soap.

As we've seen, the whole of the Land was considered holier than any other place on earth, and as we might expect, even well beyond the reach of Jerusalem and its Temple the landscape had the baths to prove it. Sepphoris alone had more than twenty, some public, some in private homes. Tiny Nazareth is believed to have had one—one bath for about 400 people. A Galilean town to the north of Sepphoris known as Yodefat had at least two private *miqwaoth*, and on the other side of the Sea of Galilee, an inland town called Gamla is believed to have had two or three.[19] The notable exception, of course, is Capernaum, where there were no baths to speak of. The explanation is clear: Ritual purity and basic physical cleanliness were handled in the very same living water of the Sea of Galilee.

It's not clear that the baths throughout Galilee operated exactly like the ones in and around Jerusalem. Indeed, had people living in Jerusalem or the Judean countryside—to say nothing of the inhabitants of Qumran, the Essenes, who have provided archaeologists with a "rich trove" of ritual baths—had any of these people ever seen the baths of Galilee, they would have certainly had some concerns. That is to say, those groups might have said that the Galileans were "doing it wrong" when it came to bathing. Typical Galilean *miqwaoth*, for instance, didn't have the two pools or the two entrances. Chiseling them into the bedrock in the first place, then carving out steps, plastering them over and over, and finally devising a system for collecting and diverting rainwater—well, that would have been difficult enough for unskilled laborers looking for a little purity when they needed it. Regardless of whether someone in Jerusalem believed a Nazarene was "doing it wrong," what all

---

19. I could go on, but suffice it to say that archaeologists have scoured Galilee and found first-century *miqwaoth* in no less than six other towns.

that hard work making baths means to us is that the Nazarene was, as Jonathan Reed says, at least "doing it." And he kept doing it.

Until, archaeologists tell us, he stopped doing it. They all stopped. After year 70 there were no more baths built in Palestine. And when the baths disappeared from Palestine, we can be sure it's because the people who depended on them for purity disappeared first—starting, of course, with those at the purest spot in the world.

VI

HEALTH IN YEAR ONE

The healthy have no use for a doctor, but the sick do.

—LUKE 5:31

First-century worries about purity were never going to end with where you lived or what you ate or when you took a bath. And although those concerns were central to life in year one, they probably aren't where most of us today would think to start when talking about whether someone was, for lack of a better word, contaminated. If we had to name one figure from the first century who's made his way down through history as representative of the worst kind of foulness imaginable, it's unlikely to be the guy who simply touched a dead body.[1] Just as unlikely

---

1. Case in point: No one remembers Joseph of Arimathea, the man responsible for taking Jesus down off the cross, for any defilement he may have sopped up from the corpse he touched.

would be the woman having her period. It's also certainly not the Essene breaking the rules with a Saturday morning bowel movement, or even the soldier trudging off to sleep outside of camp after having a wet dream. None of these come so immediately to mind[2] as a person described in the book of Leviticus: "[A] man shall have in the skin of his flesh a swelling, a scab, or bright spot, and it be in the skin of his flesh like the spots of leprosy." That's right—no matter how you look at it, the most disgusting man in the first century was the leper.[3]

Before getting too far ahead of ourselves, we should probably clear up a few things about what lepers and leprosy would have meant in the first century. To begin, the disease wasn't what you probably think. Indeed, if we're going to concern ourselves now with sick people, their doctors, and first-century health and healing in general, we should prepare ourselves to see that things are often not what we expect. On the one hand, the physical difficulties that came with being a leper wouldn't have been quite as terrible as we imagine. What gets translated in the Bible as "leprosy," from the Hebrew word *sāra'at* or the Greek work *lepra*, is not modern leprosy at all, but, as J. D. Crossan puts it, "several diseases, all of which involved a rather repulsive scaly or flaking skin condition—for

---

2. And, of course, some don't come to mind at all. Who, for example, besides perhaps the writer of Deuteronomy or a Boy Scout, has the imagination or resourcefulness to devise a game plan for getting out of camp undetected after a nocturnal emission?

3. Or maybe, since I've hinted before at the spectacular and gruesome death of King Herod, we should consider him in the running for the first century's MOST DISGUST-ING MAN award. (I'd probably give it to him.) But for the moment we're talking about popular images from year one, things most of us already know about, and in those terms the leper wins, hands down.

example, psoriasis, eczema, or any fungus infection of the skin."[4] This is not to make light of the discomfort caused by any of the skin disorders Crossan identifies by name, only to say that leprosy, as we know it, is typically characterized by wildly disfigured limbs that, at least in the popular imagination, are prone to falling off.[5] In contrast, all these first-century afflictions, it's important to note, would have been uncomfortable but temporary. Modern leprosy, caused by *Mycobacterium laprae*, a bacillus not actually observed by a physician until 1868, seems to have been known in the first century as *elephas* or *elephantiasis*.[6] And there's no actual evidence

---

4. Crossan, whose name we've seen a good number of times already, has spent a lot of time thinking and writing about healing in the first century, mainly because Jesus, Crossan's main subject of interest, is understood by many to have been a great and, indeed, magical healer. The technical term for such a person is a thaumaturge. Once again, though, our purpose is not to understand what life was like for Jesus, or even to speculate on the medical treatments he may or may not have been involved with. But that said, most people would agree that if stories about Jesus' life belong anywhere in these pages, it's probably here, where we're concerned with healing.

5. A new discovery has confirmed the earliest written account of modern leprosy in a piece of Hindu sacred text known as the *Atharva Veda*, dating from before the first millennium BCE; American anthropologist Gwen Robbins and several colleagues have found a 4,000-year-old skeleton in northwestern India whose skull has eroded in ways that are consistent with leprosy (Wade, May 26, 2009; Robbins et al., 2009). Other ancient written accounts include one from the sixth century BCE in south Asia and another from China a few centuries later: "[A villager] C has no eyebrows; the bridge of the nose is destroyed; his nasal cavity is collapsed; if you prick his nose, he does not sneeze; . . . [the] soles of both feet are defective and are suppurating in one place; his hands have no hair; I ordered him to shout and . . . his voice was hoarse. It is leprosy" (McLeod and Yates, 152–53). In this case, the description sounds nothing at all like the skin disorders described in Leviticus. We're clearly talking about very different diseases.

6. According to professors Katrina C. D. McLeod and Robin D. S. Yates, "The earliest extant Western description of low-resistance leprosy is that of Celsus (25 B.C.–A.D. 37), who called the disease elephantiasis as did Pliny (A.D. 23–79). The latter claimed that it had only appeared in Italy about a hundred years earlier" (McLeod and Yates, 152). Moreover, what we call *elephantiasis* today, a disease now famously associated

that anyone in first-century Palestine was ever infected by those bacteria. Just as archaeologists have been unable to find any pig bones in excavations of first-century Palestine, no human bones showing telltale signs of leprosy have turned up either.

(Still, I want to be clear. There is no question that some unfortunate people did develop those repulsive skin disorders described in Leviticus; a dry climate, abusive sand, and unreliable ways to keep even base-level clean were all partly to blame. And, having cleared up the confusion between modern leprosy and ancient *lepra*, for convenience' sake we'll just go on calling those unfortunate people lepers.)

It's safe to say that what the Law required of a leper is, unlike the actual condition itself, somewhat common knowledge. How we imagine the first-century leper probably has more to do with his status as an outcast than with anything we might know about the disease, or those varieties of diseases, itself. Take, for instance, the "old ex-leper" from Monty Python's satire of the life of Jesus, *The Life of Brian*. Though he appears in what can only be described as glisteningly good health—cured, as he says, by Jesus—he's still living as an outcast and a beggar. The illness is gone and yet the lifestyle remains. Or, well, working would just not be as easy as begging, the man suggests (after which we're meant to laugh). Now, explaining the joke is not my point here. My point is that if the character of the first-century *ex*-leper is one we can immediately

---

with Joseph "The Elephant Man" Merrick, should not be confused with either ancient or modern leprosy. And to further complicate matters, nor, it seems, should we think that Merrick had the disease he was named for. He had something called the "Proteus syndrome" (Tibbles and Cohen, 683–85).

identify—again, without any explanation necessary—then the leper himself must have some basic hold on our imaginations.

Once the itching started or your skin began flaking or developing sores or coming up scabby, well, that's when the treatment would have begun. And, as you may know, the typical treatment for *lepra* went something like this:

> The person who has the leprous disease shall wear torn clothes and let the hair of his head be disheveled; and he shall cover his upper lip and cry out, "Unclean, unclean." He shall remain unclean as long as he has the disease; he is unclean.[7] He shall live alone; his dwelling shall be outside the camp.[8]

What's most obvious about this approach to "the leprous disease" is that it couldn't be the leper who was treated for his illness, but the community he belonged to—a fact that would have been devastating to the man sent to live "outside the camp." As we've seen before when talking about not just family life and the economy, but also the rule of the Empire and its increasing control over the food and the land, losing the stability of a traditional Jewish home was as bad as it could get.

Lepra was a "condition of ritual impurity," as some authors

---

7. *Okay, Leviticus, we get it—he's unclean.*

8. Leviticus 14, the very next chapter, actually describes a much lengthier treatment involving the slaughter of one bird over fresh water and the dipping of another bird in the blood of the dead bird. The whole ritual, which lasts more than a week, gets exceedingly complicated and involves the purification of the house, as well. But let it be known, this treatment only begins after a priest finds that "the disease is healed in the leprous person."

have called it, that affected not just you, but your house and clothing, too. The worry of a leper was less that he'd lose a toe or an arm and more that he'd lose his life as he knew it. It wasn't death that concerned him most, but exile.[9] His impurity and discomfort were compounded by instability; a man with the flaky skin of psoriasis wandered around homeless—perhaps begging—while his house was not fit to return to; he tore his clothes and told the world he was unclean.

Not that the leper would have actually had to say anything. Everyone around him would have known he had the "leprous disease" just by looking at him. The torn clothes and all that shouting seems like a little overkill. And, while there were first-century physicians—most notably, the Gospel writer Luke—it usually didn't require a doctor to tell whether you were sick or not.[10] Unfortunately, whether you were sick or well wasn't exactly like what we saw when considering who was clean or

---

9. We can assume he would have seen, and probably even experienced, the sores and flaking skin as temporary, and probably not actually life-threatening, anyway. That said, there's no telling how long a leper would stay a leper, and what impact even a few weeks outside the camp would have on your standing, or your family's standing, within the community.

10. This is probably just as true today as it was then. We tend to know when we're sick, even if we don't know exactly what it is we're sick with. Indeed, in recent years we've grown more aware of our symptoms than ever before, in large part because of a brand-new ailment called "cyberchondria," defined in 2008 as "unfounded escalation of concerns about common symptomatology" (White and Horvitz, November 1, 2008). We've all done it. With the world of medicine just an Internet search away, every headache suddenly means a brain tumor, every muscle twitch, an early sign of ALS. Researchers have referred to this as "a user's predisposition to escalate versus to seek more reasonable explanations for ailments." In other words, when it comes to our metastasizing brain tumor or a life cut short just like Lou Gehrig's, we're almost always wrong.

dirty, where looks could be deceiving. In Tobit's case, remember, what made him dirty and impure was not the bird droppings all over his face, but the fact that he'd touched a dead body, which would have left no physical evidence at all. The everyday filth of first-century Palestine, just as in Tobit's day, was just too pervasive, and water too scarce, to stay on top of—which was, in the end, really no big deal. The most important bath you could take was a ritual one. And while the ritual bath might have had washed some of the dirt off, you could look a little filthy and still be perfectly clean. What the squawking leper tells us is that the same cannot be said about health. You could not look sick and not actually *be* sick. Even worse, this made you just as impure as if you'd gone ahead and eaten a pork chop.

And if all this weren't bad enough, the leper had to deal with the fact that the cause of his illness would have been as obvious to everyone—including himself—as the illness itself. Once again, disease was not a private matter. And at the root of the public face of disease was the notion that, as medical historian Roy Porter has said, "[c]ertain maladies were associated with the Almighty's punishments for sin." *Lepra* was one of those illnesses.

Sure, exactly what sinning you'd done may have remained between you and God, but when those boils started breaking out on your skin, there was no hiding the fact that you'd done something worth the punishment—presumably, even if you hadn't.[11]

---

11. This is a point the writer Susan Sontag has made about what she calls "putative notions of disease" that persist even today (especially with regard to cancer and HIV/AIDS). "Patients who are instructed that they have, unwittingly, caused their disease," she writes, "are also being made to feel that they have deserved it" (Sontag, 56).

And while nowadays we tend to treat even *deserving* sick people,[12] in the first century treating the community—that is, kicking the leper out of town—was really the best thing any physician could do. As Roy Porter concludes, "Such polluting diseases were curable by the Lord alone." Which meant that from the leper's perspective—as if all *that* weren't bad enough[13]—he had to deal not only with the fact that his discomfort and pain were his own fault and everyone knew it, but also with the possibility that if anyone were to help him, that person might be sinning just the same. Catching someone's disease would have meant catching someone's sin. In a world crawling with demons, it would have meant getting the devil on your back.

The very suggestion that anyone should be treated for a health problem like *lepra* was always an open question back then. And given what we've seen so far about how central God was in everyday life, this first-century concern should actually make a certain kind of sense—even if it's not how most of us think of illness today. Health in year one was almost never about what usually seems most important these days: *How are you feeling?* The better question to ask might have been: *How has God made you feel?* Or better still, *Why has God made you feel that way?* And believing there were divine answers to questions like these would have led people to wonder what right they had to interfere with the work of God. We see that even as

---

12. Well, the insured ones, anyway.
13. The badness, we see, just continues to mount for the leper.

late as the eleventh century CE, the great rabbi Rashi was still asking, "How is it that God smites and man heals?"

All of this is to say that we should imagine that Jewish physicians—even, presumably, Luke—have essentially been looking for God's permission to heal from the beginning. And God had, in their experience, been a little stingy with the go-ahead. Those people who took an interest in healing during the first century would have known the biblical fate of King Asa (ca. 914–874 BCE) just as well as someone practicing *onanism* would have known the biblical fate of poor Onan. Suffering from severe foot disease within a year of making some foolish political decisions, Asa, we're told, "did not seek the Lord, but sought help from physicians." And as any first-century physician would have known, that would turn out to be the king's last foolish decision. As the religious historian Géza Vermes notes, "Needless to add, [Asa] soon died."

The fate of King Asa might explain what Vermes calls the near complete silence in the Bible "on the subject of professional healing"—something that might strike us, who are interested in professional healing, as a little frustrating. Because, unlike in other chapters where we could look to archaeology for answers about what a house might have looked like or for evidence of what languages were used in the *agora*, when it comes to health, archaeology doesn't have much to say. No one left behind any stethoscopes or a first-century forceps; there's no such thing as a year one waiting room. And even where we're positive they did things we might today call surgical—say, circumcision—we'd be hoping against hope to turn up a cutting instrument bearing the same edge as a twenty-first-century scalpel. But the larger point here is that the very little we can know about the practice of healing in first-century Palestine has to come from books—most notably, the "almost completely silent" Bible. Although, where medicine is concerned, if there's one thing the Bible is clear about, it's that there was, as Vermes says, a "divine monopoly" on healing.

Still, what we mean by "divine monopoly" is perhaps itself an open question. It was a debated point among the people in the first century (and a point that's been debated continually ever since). Certainly, looking at the Bible one can find a Jewish tradition where, according to one rabbi today, healing is actually considered a mandate rooted in the "ethical thrust of Leviticus and Deuteronomy"—a type of ethics that should be seen as "unconditional." In other words, there's some real sense behind considering healing alongside the religious imperatives everyone felt to welcome the stranger (so long as he's a Jew), care for orphans and widows (so long as they're Jewish), or, as we saw with Tobit, to feed the poor (so long as they're . . . well, you get the point). Those same books where we find such commandments, as we've seen, shaped the lives of those living in first-century Palestine. And so, the tension between what God intended when he punished someone with *lepra*, say, and what a physician could do to treat or cure suffering and disease is something they felt every bit in year one. It's something Rashi felt in the eleventh century, and it's a tension we can still feel today, to some respects, in lawsuits filed against members of religious groups who refuse medical treatment for their children, because, in the words of a former Christian Scientist, "we knew that once we went to the doctor, we'd be cut off from God"—just like King Asa.

Yet where healing in the first century was concerned, this tension between the will of God and the work of man was able to find some release—although the balance professional healers achieved in order to treat disease would have been delicate. Vermes calls it a "compromise" and imagines the ancient Jewish doctor as a tightrope walker; indeed, he was working against the general assumption that "to refer certain matters of health to a priest was a duty; to seek the help of a prophet was an act of religion; and to visit the doctor was an act of impiety." And so, doctors would have been sure to treat only those people who had properly prepared for their visit—that is, those who had prayed, confessed the sins that were plaguing them, and then, as a Catholic might do today in the privacy of a confessional, committed to never sinning again. Then, once the patient arrived, the doctor would prepare himself for the exam, which wouldn't necessarily have even involved hand washing. Instead, the physician said prayers of his own, asking God to reveal to him the illness—even if it was already obvious—and to direct him to a cure. That cure might have come through concoctions of any number of plants and herbs, even spit or olive oil, that we should always remember were, as Vermes says, "divinely ordained." Successful doctors of the time did the work of God. And ultimately, they lived out the maxim of a first-century Jewish physician: "Professional knowledge is an additional asset to the healer's essential requisite, holiness."

What this maxim seems to suggest is that the holier the man, the more effective he should be as a healer. And this was partly true. On the one hand, a priest would have been limited in what he could do in his role as a medicine man. His duties would have amounted to little more than simple diagnoses of *lepra*, say, or helping purify someone after childbirth, menstruation, or a v.d.[14]—not bad, but not exactly what you'd call a cure for cancer.

That said, priests weren't the only men of God in those days. And where health was concerned, the priests' interests would have always been more in line with keeping the community safe, whole, and pure. As we'll see, priests were part of the religious institution, hardly inclined toward rocking the boat by absorbing, or *catching*, as it were, impurity themselves.[15]

There were also the prophets, often known for their big, anti-institutional personalities and a tendency to mix and meddle with sickly types. Of these two types of godly men, the prophet was more naturally—and if you're inclined to think this way, supernaturally—a healer. They were, in a sense, men of the people, often acting "as moral and social critics of kings and priests," and their connection to God was more immediate and direct, not mediated through the rituals of the Jewish religious institution. And so the prophet's power to heal came directly from God as well. They were what we call charismatics.

---

14. Vermes notes that the "sundry purificatory rites" that priests administered in the wake of any of these causes of ritual impurity were not what we might consider medicine, but involved "medical overtones" (Vermes, 59).

15. Just for example, the treatment of the leper would have had the official priestly seal of approval.

The most famous charismatic healers from history found a place in the Bible, and their healings were renowned in year one. Elijah, Elisha, and Isaiah had in their own times revived people from apparent death, cured a leper with a ritual bath, and restored the health of a king using only a "lump of figs." And in the first century, there was no reason to believe such things weren't possible still. Indeed, they were happening. All it took was the right charismatic with the right connection to God, and without doubt, these people existed—performing exorcisms, forgiving sins, and making people clean. They traded in miracles.

Now, with that single word—miracles—we've finally arrived on what some might consider shaky ground. (Indeed, I find the ground rather shaky myself.) But there's no way around it. In the first century, healing was a religious practice and God was capable of anything. And if you think about it, where the greater of two evils was the embarrassment and exile that went along with some mildly aggravating skin disorders, perhaps the greater good that God could do would be to forgo sending you into the wilderness at all. Maybe the miracle was simply to be forgiven and welcomed back, even while you still showed symptoms of sin. According to anthropologist Leon Eisenberg, "The very limitations of their technology kept indigenous healers more responsive to the extra-biological aspects of illness, for it was chiefly those aspects they could manipulate." Which is basically to say that healers working with spittle, a lump of figs, a purifying river, and some mud would have done their best work—the work of God—when they looked past the disease itself and saw a way to introduce the sick sinner back into his home. (Talk about a bedside manner.) From this perspective, it's possible to imagine how these particular kinds of healers—most notably those prophets who would have found the treatment of the leper to be not just inadequate but very likely unholy—may have operated in the first century without believing in magic or miracles. Or it's possible to imagine that the magic of a miracle has less to do with breaking the laws of physics and more with breaking the laws of society.[16]

Despite your take on what happens when someone performs a miracle—and it's not impossible to imagine that both the wizardly and nonwizardly versions happened side by side—it's been said that ancient healers would have approached their work in one of three ways, in every case, of course, by tapping into the power of God. Some healers petitioned God for help. In other words, they prayed. Others believed they were acting as a mediator for God. They had no healing power of their own;

---

16. As I've already said, J. D. Crossan has written a lot, and very convincingly, about first-century healing (cf. footnote 4 in this chapter). This idea, for example, that restoring someone to health in year one might have primarily involved what he calls the "entire psychological [and] . . . entire social dimension of the phenomenon," well, not surprisingly, that basically comes from him. Now, in coming up with his ideas about how a leper might have been "healed" in the first century, Crossan relies on the fields of medical anthropology and comparative ethnomedicine, which draw distinctions between "*curing a disease*" and "*healing an illness.*" A disease, in today's terms, is the biological or psychological malfunction, e.g., your skin flares up. An illness is something more complicated, and involves the meaning of the disease and the way the disease affects your social standing, e.g., your skin flares up, you understand you completely deserve it, and you become an outcast. What all of this goes to show is that the treatment we saw in Leviticus for *lepra* would have done absolutely nothing to cure the disease, but would have made the illness much, much worse (Crossan, *Jesus*, 75–82; Crossan, *The Birth of Christianity*, 293–94).

God worked *through* them. The third kind of healer was perhaps the least common and most dangerous—both to himself in the face of religious authority, and also to the sin, or demons, he sought to expel. This was the sort of healer who, as religious historian Werner Kahl puts it, "incorporates the healing power personally, functioning as the *means* of God's healing activity." And as you can probably understand, operating this way—essentially healing *as God*—might have flown in the face of a religious authority whose entire, well, *authority* rested on there being only one God with whom they maintained a special relationship.

And so, as we might expect, there were probably very few of this kind of first-century healer. By my count, there may have been only one. But, as I said at the beginning, this just isn't a book about him.

VII

R-E-S-P-E-C-T IN YEAR ONE

A prophet is not dishonored when not in his own town
or home.

—MATTHEW 13:57

More than once we've witnessed the kind of local pride that, in some ways, Rome made it their business to keep in check during the first century. No Jew, no matter how important or wise or brutal, was allowed to get too big for his own britches.[1] Even someone as powerful as King Herod understood he could only get *so* prideful. His rule in Jerusalem, for instance, began in 37 BCE with the massacre of some forty-five enemies of Rome, proud members of the outgoing dynasty still clinging to Jewish independence, an

---

1. Some people would offer John the Baptist and Jesus, both killed under the authority of Rome, as cases in point; unsurprisingly, we also have other examples.

ambition presumably abandoned by Herod. If that massacre alone wasn't enough to dash the spirits of the remaining Hasmonean loyalists, Herod sent Antigonus, their former king, off to the Roman Mark Antony[2] in chains. In other words, Herod, a Jew, performed the work of the Roman Empire and curried its favor by turning over the very popular king of the Jews. (It goes without saying that he also helped himself in the process.) Antigonus's surrender to the Roman army commander Sosius—who had handed Antigonus over to Herod—is a bit of ancient comedy as Josephus tells it: "At this point Antigonus, paying no regard to his past or to his present position, came down from his Palace and fell at Sosius's feet. The Roman, not in the least moved by his changed situation, laughed uproariously and called him Antigone." This is only funny if you understand that "Antigone" is a girl's name, and even then, it's not really *that* funny. Still Josephus continues, "But he [Sosius] did not treat him like a woman and let him go free: he put him in fetters and kept him in custody." Again, via Herod, Antony then had Antigonus beheaded. He died, as Josephus writes, "as such a coward deserved—by the axe." (Clearly, Josephus was a man who knew what side his bread was buttered on.)

What's remarkable about this moment is that to this point, beheading a king was something Rome was never known to have done.[3] Josephus explains elsewhere, in his work *The Antiq-*

---

2. Of course, this is the same kingmaker Mark Antony—"Friends, Romans, countrymen"—who helped install Herod in the first place.

3. This allows us to see the mocking of Jesus with a crown of thorns and his crucifixion as "King of the Jews" in a slightly new light. It's as if Rome was telling him, *If*

uities of the Jews, by quoting the Greek historian Strabo: "Antony ordered Antigonus the Jew to be brought to Antioch, and there to be beheaded; and this Antony seems to me to have been the very first man who beheaded a king, as supposing he could no other way bend the minds of the Jews so as to receive Herod." Strabo was right, of course: Herod had opponents throughout Palestine whose minds needed to be bent. But one also has to ask if Antony didn't also have in mind bending Herod's own mind in a certain direction—letting him know, *Look, I killed one king, King Herod; don't think I won't do it again.*

In their own ways, the events surrounding Antigonus's execution are no less telling than the execution itself. To begin with, Herod seemed to be entirely aware of just how fragile the political situation he inherited was, even while Antigonus still had his wits, and his head, about him. Not only had the might of Rome and the influence of Antony installed Herod as king, but three years later, they also helped him wrest control of Jerusalem, the heart of the Jewish world and the last remaining stronghold of the Hasmoneans. As we've said before, to the winners go the spoils: not just Herod, of course, but his powerful friends, as well. Something the king would have known instinctively. First, as Josephus tells it, "the alien masses"—that is, the Romans—"were determined to see the Temple and the sacred things inside." What's more, the Roman commander Sosius was equally determined to allow his soldiers to loot the city—"it was

---

you were really and truly a king we might give this execution a little more thought. You're obviously not. So, up you go!

only right to let the men pillage," Josephus insists. Confronting that first threat, against the Temple, Herod drew a line in the sand, perhaps out of respect for his fellow Jews, perhaps out of respect for his God. He "appealed to some, threatened others, and drove yet others back by force of arms." Under no condition would Rome enter the Holy of Holies.[4] (Or, in any event, not until they destroyed it about a hundred years later.)

Money, though, is an infinitely more fungible commodity than holiness. So when faced with the looting, Herod took a more practical, diplomatic, and personally costly approach. Rather than allow Romans to strip Jerusalem of both its wealth and its men—that is, they planned to both loot and murder, leaving Herod "the king of a desert"—he paid "the whole army out of his own pocket," beginning with Sosius. How's that for an ancient lesson in winning friends and influencing people?

If what led up to Antigonus's execution reveals the delicate balance Herod maintained in the early years of his reign—how, in Josephus's words, Herod mastered not only his enemies but also his "foreign allies"—what followed the murder of his rival tells us just how much his loyalty to Rome may really have meant. Enter Cleopatra,[5] the Egyptian queen Mark Antony fell so famously, and disastrously, in love with. As Josephus tells it,

---

4. Josephus writes that Herod thought "victory more terrible than defeat if such people got a glimpse within the Veil" (Josephus, *The Jewish War*, 74). Herod seems to have believed somewhere in his heart of hearts that the mysterious power of God was actually more to worry about than the military power of Rome.

5. Of "Ah, women, women! Come; we have no friend / But resolution, and the briefest end."

Cleopatra "ruined" Antony—his passion and desire for her were limitless—and in her pursuit of the riches held in the corner of the Roman Empire known as Palestine, she "worked in secret" to have Herod put to death. All the while, Herod sent gifts and at great expense became a tenant himself, renting lands that Antony had sliced off his territory and handed over to Cleopatra. Whether Josephus is telling a story squarely is always debatable—and we know these ancient writers have no love for women. But what he tells us about the end of Herod's relationship with Antony suggests that the king had always impressed the Roman. "Antony," Josephus concludes, "was sober enough to realize that one part of [Cleopatra's] demands—the killing of honest men and famous kings—was utterly immoral." (Apparently, the late beheaded Antigonus wasn't honest or famous enough for this system of ethics to apply to him.) And so ultimately, Herod's life was saved by his respect for Rome. (Of course, there is a fine line between respect and fear.) But in the end, Antony "cut [Herod] to the heart by withdrawing his friendship."

Respect for God, for fellow Jews, friends and lovers, enemies and allies, Rome itself—this all meant a lot in year one, and how respect played out tended to be fairly predictable. Lines like the one Herod drew between the Romans and the Temple were deep and lasting.[6] His outpost at the Mediterranean port city of Caesarea Maritima, on the other hand, tells a very different

---

6. And given the depth of the line he drew when he took over Jerusalem, Herod's bizarre decision, presumably near the end of his reign, to mount the golden eagle on the Temple makes sense—perhaps more sense now—in the way we've already suggested: As the end approached, the king lost his mind.

story about respect. To begin with, the city was named for Caesar. If that wasn't enough, to underscore its direct and obvious orientation to Rome, Caesarea was dominated by a temple to the goddess Roma and the emperor Augustus, which, according to Josephus, housed huge statues honoring the Roman deities. (I say "according to Josephus" because those statues haven't yet been discovered. That said, archaeologists have uncovered statues of the emperor Trajan, who ruled from 98 to 117 CE, and his successor Hadrian, both outside of our time frame, perhaps, but their presence, as Crossan and Reed attest, "offer concrete evidence of the imperial cult and emperor worship there." These cults simply did not exist in Jerusalem.) And while the statues alone might tell of just how respectful Herod's Caesarea was to Rome (and even what kind of shrewd flip-flopper a king could be), Crossan and Reed see the existence of another piece of ancient stone to be more indicative of the real influence the emperor would have had during the dynasty that began with Herod the Great.

In 1962, Italian archaeologists discovered a Latin inscription on the back of a stone used during the renovation of the theater in Caesarea during the fourth century. The inscription turns out to name a very important figure in the history of Christianity: Pontius Pilate, the Roman authority who oversaw the execution of Jesus. Crossan and Reed tell us that most—indeed, "too many"—people who study and write about things like this have focused on the fact that this inscription, dating to the first century and naming Pontius Pilate, even identifying him as the "prefect of Judea," confirms the existence of an important player in the Christian Gospels version of *Who's Who of First-Century*

Palestine. (That said, few people had ever doubted that Pilate was a Roman prefect[7] during this time.) Crossan and Reed, however, would point out a few other things about this ancient find: First, beyond simply naming Pilate and proclaiming his title, the inscription also indicates that he was responsible for erecting, in Caesarea, a building where the stone was originally installed. It was called the Tiberium, named for the emperor during Pilate's time—which means Jesus' time, too—Tiberius. What's more, the authors conclude, since the inscription was written in Latin, "a language few there could understand much less read," the story it would have told "even to the dullest mind" was "that Rome and its representatives stood at the top of the social pyramid and held absolute control over the land." Crossan and Reed aren't pulling any punches here; when they refer to "the land" they mean the entirety of what Jews believed was "the Land." Though the person we've been calling a typical first-century Jew might not ever have made it to see Pilate's inscription in Caesarea—nor, can we imagine, would he have wanted to, what with all those graven images around—most visitors making their way into Palestine via the Mediterranean Sea would have read the writing on the wall, so to speak: ROME OWNS THIS, TOO.[8]

---

7. Crossan and Reed tell us that the inscription helps settle a long-standing debate over Pilate's official Roman title. In the end, though, the authors insist that the debate itself deals with "a point of Roman legal minutiae and of little general interest" (Crossan and Reed, 60). You may be pleased to know that I agree, and so, for our purposes, the debate stops here.

8. Crossan and Reed put it this way: "*Rome Rules!*" (Crossan and Reed, 61).

There's some indication, even in what we've seen so far, that respect went both ways between the Jews and the Romans. It's evident, at least anecdotally, in the fact that Pilate didn't build the Tiberium in Jerusalem but in Caesarea. This is not to say that Roman influence wasn't felt even in the heart of the Land; Pilate was, after all, the Roman prefect of Judea, stationed in its capital of Jerusalem.

Through Herod's influence originally, that city had become a model of high urban living, complete with a Roman theater, a hippodrome—which hosted Roman-style chariot races complete with raucous crowds—an amphitheater, a massive council building known as the *bouleuterion*, great streets, marketplaces, and a brand-new system of aqueducts. Rome was famous for its aqueducts. Herod even built a palace there and named it for Mark Antony, calling it "Antonia"—something a king could get away with that a prefect perhaps could not. Even so, with the Temple on its mount, the focal point of every citizen and visitor alike, the public face of Jerusalem remained always Jewish. As we've seen, to further shore up the respect of his fellow Jews, when Herod married a second time, he chose Mariamme, the granddaughter of a Hasmonean king. A few years later he even brought out of exile a former High Priest of the same dysfunctional dynastic family, Hyrcanus II, who'd been sent off to Babylonia four years earlier.[9] (Although for

---

9. The exile of Hyrcanus, the former king and High Priest, is more complicated than what we can get into here. Still, we can say this much: Antigonus, who, as we've

the record, before Herod died, fearing the pride of the remaining Hasmoneans—and what Lee Levine calls their "residual popularity" among the people—he ended up killing not just Hyrcanus II, but his daughter Alexandra, too, not to mention two of her children, the High Priest Aristobulus III and, yes, his own wife Mariamme. Once again we see here the fine line between respect and fear—and in Herod's case, downright paranoia.)

It's true that the earliest stories from Jerusalem of Antigonus, Antony, and the murderous Herod all predate year one by more than thirty-five years; and, the unearthed sculptures associated with imperial cult in Caesarea would have been erected no earlier than the beginning of the second century. Still, what all this tells us—most specifically Pilate's inscription—is that keeping some local pride in check would have meant allowing other local pride to flourish. Where Rome was concerned, this began with installing Herod as king, continued when Caesar Augustus assumed direct control of Palestine in 6 CE, and concluded with the war that's been hanging over our heads this entire book. And for all that time, by and large, the Romans let the Jews of the Empire live as Jews and exhibit their Jewishness, going so far as to mint those special coins for them to use and allow them their ritual baths. One could argue over the reasons

---

seen, went down in history as the first king ever beheaded by the Romans, initially gained the throne by usurping his uncle Hyrcanus in 40 BCE. Not of a mind to kill him, but most certainly inclined to protect both the throne and the office of the High Priest, Antigonus, anticipating the unorthodox pugilistic techniques of heavyweight champion Mike Tyson, bit at least some of his uncle's ears off. High Priests, Josephus explains, had to be "physically perfect" (Josephus, *The Jewish War*, 63).

for this sort of tolerance. The less cynical among us might say that, in general, Romans truly respected the Jews—in large part, as religion writer Karen Armstrong has said, because "their religion was known to be of great antiquity." Armstrong goes on, characterizing the first century as a time of great ethical and religious exchange and experimentation: "People in the Roman empire were searching for new religious solutions; monotheistic ideas were in the air, and local gods were increasingly seen as mere manifestations of a more encompassing divinity. The Romans were drawn to the high moral character of Judaism." Some Romans went so far as to convert, which would have required them to be circumcised. "Those who were understandably reluctant," Armstrong concludes, "often became honorary members of the synagogues, known as the 'Godfearers.'"[10]

There's no denying that in certain circles Armstrong's story about the Empire's respect for first-century Jews would have rung true. Some scholars have even claimed that there were members of the Flavian dynasty, the Roman family who assumed control of the Empire during the Jewish rebellion, who actually converted to Judaism near the end of the first century.[11]

---

10. There's that word "fear" again—remarkably, in this case, part in parcel of the Romans' respect for the Jews. It seems that fear, like respect, ran both ways, too.

11. Armstrong mentions this possibility, and there's even been some speculation that these two Flavians, Clemens, the emperor Domitian's cousin, and his wife Domitilla, may have actually become Christians. In any event, they were charged with "drift[ing] into Jewish ways" (Cotton and Eck, 44–45)—which, we'll see, would have included Christianity—and Clemens was eventually executed for it. What seems more likely than any full religious conversion, however, is that Clemens and Domitilla became honorary Jews (Armstrong, 71). It seems as though Clemens, a Godfearer, might have fared better if he had feared Rome, instead.

Ultimately, though, it's hard to ignore the fact that tolerating the Jewishness of the Jews allowed the Empire to accrue more power and more riches, which along the way allowed some individual Jews and their families to do very well for themselves. Others, though, particularly those living in the countryside, would have fared worse.

This is what we've seen among the Galileans indentured under the rule of Antipas, who followed in his father's footsteps not only with regard to his architectural vision but also, necessarily, his love and respect for Rome. Sepphoris and Tiberias, Galilee's major cities, may have, like Jerusalem, lacked the statues of Caesarea. Even so, we've seen Latin measures in the marketplace and talked about Antipas's Roman-style architecture and city planning. As the century wore on, Sepphorians even had their own small version of a Roman theater, complete with what was known as the *vomitoria*, passages from the mid-level sections that allowed the lower classes to pour in and out down below, without mingling with the city's elites—many of whom had seats in the theater inscribed with their names. (Living in the days of $2,500 seats and personal luxury suites at the ballpark, this public expression of wealth should come as no surprise.) Those well-to-do theatergoers came and went through totally separate entrances called *parodoi*, a name that lacks the imagination of *vomitoria*[12]—*the* singular *parados* simply means "a way by"—but also shares a root with the word

---

12. A name meant to call to mind just what you'd expect: The theater essentially puked out poor people.

"paranoid," a fitting description of people who couldn't bring themselves to share even a passageway with ancient lower-class groundlings.

On the face of it, the rich seemed to have had a very hard time respecting the poor. The feeling was probably mutual. Even among fellow Jews.

Yes, I've said before that there was a kind of national pride that would have trumped expressions of local pride among Jews in the first century. That is, you and your fellow Jews, rich or poor, were members of the chosen people. Period. And everyone knew it. (That said, there was likewise that sense that all Jews are chosen, but some Jews are more chosen than others.) In the ways that ultimately mattered most—i.e., the ways of purity and impurity—non-Jews were simply not as respectable, to put it mildly, as Jews.

There's a reason, for instance, why a story about a "good" Samaritan is worth telling during the first century. Samaritans were considered unclean "foreigners" in the eyes of any first-century Jew, despite the fact that Samaria, or Samaratis (as it was also known), was the region of Palestine located directly between Judea in the south and Galilee in the north. Though the two groups shared a common ancestry—dating to before the reign of King Solomon (d. 935 BCE)—ever since they'd maintained what's been called a "simmering hatred." Samaritans read a different Torah and gathered in a different Temple. Their land was not part of *the Land*. The animosity between the groups was mainly expressed through insults and "cutting irony," in the words of one historian. He continues, "The Samaritans were called a herd, an odd collection of undesirables, and it was not allowed that they had any right to call themselves a nation.[13] The name Shechem [a city in Samaria] was turned into Sychar, which means drunkenness. A widely current proverb, which is recorded in the Talmud, said that 'a piece of bread given by a Samaritan is more unclean than swine's flesh.'"

And just like the respect the Jews shared with the Romans, the suspicion and hatred of the Samaritans appears to have gone both ways as well. Once, during the first decade of the first century, for instance, a group of Samaritans took several dead bodies and scattered them throughout the cloisters of the Temple on the first night of Passover. Now, if a piece of bread handled by a Samaritan was more impure than a piece of pork, just imagine how impure those dead bodies must have been— polluted in their own right simply by being corpses, and then handled and dumped by the dread Samaritans. This is impurity times impurity: Impurity squared![14] (Needless to say, the

---

13. I don't need to mention, I suppose, that hostilities have nearly always been hottest in this part of the world between people who seem to have the most in common, not least of all a common border, or worse, a common claim on some bit of land.

14. Henri Daniel-Rops, the French historian quoted above—and as we'll see, below— exhibits not only a distinctly apologetic position when it comes to Christian history, but also a strange (and, I admit, similar) kind of gallows humor in his description of these particular events at the Temple: "What is certain is that at the time of Christ there existed an extremely violent hatred between the two groups [the Jews and the Samaritans]. It was a hatred that went as far as actions. Sometimes these were comic, such as that which perhaps took place in the very year of our Lord's birth, when the Samaritans threw human bones into the sanctuary of the Temple just before the Passover" (Daniel-Rops, 40–41). Now, I've undoubtedly made light of the ways in which certain things became contaminated in year one—bodies, bread, and, you'll recall, the Boy Scout—but I wouldn't exactly call tossing dead people around a Temple "comic." Maybe it helps to be French.

Samaritans were not invited back to the Temple, the "good" one that Jesus talked about notwithstanding.)

There's no denying that matters of purity and national pride shaped the relationship between first-century Jews and the rest of the world. But there's a risk in making too much of this pride—call it national self-respect. Take, for instance, the conclusion of the historian we quoted above, Henri Daniel-Rops, on the matter of what he calls "the basic fact, the essential idea, without which the history, the spiritual life and even the everyday existence of Israel is incomprehensible."

> A national pride, in comparison with our own most frantic chauvinism is as nothing, filled the heart of the humblest Jew when he remembered that he belonged to the chosen race, to the people of the covenant. What did it matter that his personal lot should be commonplace, that life should treat him roughly or that the occupying Romans should trample the holy ground beneath their feet? He might be despised, but he knew very well that in common with his whole nation he had a privilege that no power on earth could take from him, the "unchanging priestly office" of which the Epistle to the Hebrews speaks.

What did it matter, indeed! For all the national pride a peasant Jew might have shared with his new landlord in the city, he still woke up every day knowing that the land he farmed was no longer his. Despite any lingering sense a poor fisherman had of being part of the "chosen race," the exact wording of the covenant, we can imagine, must have occasionally slipped his mind as he faced the officials collecting the taxes on his catch and the rent on the piece of water he fished. If it really didn't matter just how despised you were by Rome, why would Jesus, or any teacher, have encouraged his followers in Galilee with this idea: "Happy are you when they revile you and punish you and make every charge against you because of me"? National pride, it turns out, could only go so far, especially in the face of the widening inequality that accompanied Rome to Palestine. It could be said that like politics, all pride is local. And when local pride meets local pride, rivalries develop. Even among fellow Jews.

The most obvious rifts opened up along the lines we've already been talking about. You might say that first-century Palestine was set up a little like country mouse, city mouse, only with less hospitality. Suspicions were deep on both sides, and were largely rooted in whether you were able to take advantage of Rome, or Rome was able to take advantage of you. (As we've seen, in year one the city mouse would collaborate with the cat.) Cities were basically conservative places, centers of increasing wealth, commerce, political rule, and religious authority. Revolutions were the product of the countryside, where the covenant with God became less and less clear with each passing year. And as I've said, it would be a rural revolution beginning in 66 CE that would bring the end of the most important city of all. When that trap was sprung, the city mouse and the country mouse both lost their heads.

Jew vs. Roman, poor vs. rich, and country vs. city are not the only ways that people living in Palestine during the first century divided themselves up. Even within those categories there would have been subtle expressions of resentment and respect, fear and disdain that we can't even begin to imagine here. The intractable mess in current-day Palestine may, in fact, offer us some sense of just how intractable those ancient animosities would have been. Different people, different powers, and different fears, perhaps—but lines drawn in the sands of Palestine today are no more lasting and no more deep[15] than when, with all due respect, Herod faced down the Romans in Jerusalem braced by the fear of a Jewish God.

There's one final rivalry that deserves some attention. And despite all the care we've taken to suggest that relationships in year one were often a careful balance between love and hate, friend and enemy, respect and fear, this last one illustrates that subtlety is not always—or even often—animosity's strong suit. What's more, it's an enmity that should sound familiar to American ears: north vs. south.

We've bounced back and forth quite a lot now between the goings-on in Galilee in the north and Judea in the south. And as we've said time and again, these people lived very similar lives; an archaeologist would say that "religious indicators show

---

15. Although nowadays, these lines are increasingly drawn with walls that reach more than twenty-five feet into the air.

that Galileans and Judeans had much in common in their daily religious practice." The reason for this is, in fact, quite clear. Galileans have their roots in Judea. And yet, the people from the north were widely known by the epithet 'Amei Ha-aretz, or "peasants." And since the archaeological record shows that Galileans and Judeans seemed to have fairly similar religious lives—diet, purity, coins, etc.—the basis for the ridicule seems to have been class differences, even if it did on occasion strike a religious nerve, as when a Jewish leader named Yohanan ben Zakkai scolded, "Galilee, Galilee, you hate the Torah!" Ultimately, life in Galilee was largely seen by Judeans as second, even third, class. As Géza Vermes has said, they were considered "on the whole boors." Even the Galilean pronunciation of Aramaic was the subject of long and winding ridicule in the Talmud—the rabbis, it seems, got in on the fun of mocking the peasants from Galilee, too.[16]

Apart from Josephus's defense of Galileans as solid soldiers and the all-out attack on the religious authority in Jerusalem that we find in the Gospels, particularly the book of John, this rivalry seems to have been largely one-sided, at least in the historical record. The resentments of the 'Amei Ha-aretz we have

---

16. In the Gospels, Peter is identified as a follower of Jesus simply by his accent: "You are one of them, for your accent betrays you." It's even been suggested that Jesus himself, calling out in Aramaic from the cross, couldn't quite make himself clear: Eloi Eloi lama sabachtani ("My God, my God, why have you abandoned me?" [Matthew 27:46; translated by Wills, What Jesus Meant, 114]) is understood by some onlookers as an invocation of Elijah. Although Géza Vermes maintains, however, that "it would be wrong to argue . . . that he was unintelligible to the people of Jerusalem. Clarity cannot be expected of the cry of a crucified man at the point of death" (Vermes, 53–54).

to assume. (And we should assume Galilean peasants resented not just the ridicule, but as I've suggested, the class differences that fueled it.) Even so, Galileans would have seen Judea as the center of the world. And they would have made their way to Jerusalem for religious festivals as often as they could. But at the same time, the center of the world would have seemed like a half a world away. As often as they could was by no means often enough. And, though you'll have to pardon me for this, that distance—or basically, the absence of the Temple from their lives—would have made the heart grow fonder.

VIII

RELIGION IN YEAR ONE

Father,
let your name be made sacred,
let your dominion come.
Give us our bread needed for the day,
and forgive us our sins,
for we also forgive all who owe us.

—LUKE 11:2–4

From the beginning we've been interested in finding any number of answers to one thorny question: What was it like to live in first-century Palestine? For all we haven't been able to say, what seems most clear[1] is that, with no "heads" on your coins, no pig on your plate,[2] and baths designed specifically to

---

1. Apart, of course, from the taxes in chapter I and the death, we'll see, in chapter X.
2. Well, no plate to speak of, either—but now we're splitting hairs.

keep you pure in the eyes of God, if you lived in first-century Palestine, you lived what today we would almost certainly call a religious life. For a first-century Jew, though, it was just life—albeit a messy life, as we've seen.[3]

Reminders of the Jewish God were everywhere in year one. In his writing about first-century Jerusalem, archaeologist Lee Levine takes for granted what he calls a certain "religious ambience," which suggests that what we know as religion, specifically Judaism, was nothing less than the very mood and atmosphere that hung in the air. And not just in Jerusalem, but throughout the whole land. This is not to say there was a synagogue on every corner[4] the way houses of worship dot the American landscape today. What we call a house of worship (something of a misnomer in the first century, we'll see) would not have been quite so obvious back then, except for in Jerusalem, where the Temple dominated the entire city. Nor could we expect your average family to have owned personal Bible scrolls, objects that would have been practically worthless to the 97 percent of people who couldn't read, and yet so valuable and sacred where they existed that they would have been kept under lock and key.

For the record, these Bible scrolls would also have been very

---

3. Journalist Jeff Sharlet has remarked that writers who explore the religious lives of people today often find themselves "wading through the muck of the ordinary, a mudslide of the mundane, an apocalyptic swamp of What Is" (Sharlet, Manseau, et al., eds., xii–xiii). Given all the muck and mud we've seen covering the streets and rooftops, the *apocalyptic swamp* that was so much of first-century Palestine, Sharlet's claim might, in fact, be even truer in our case—indeed, literally true.

4. Much less a *corner* on every corner.

difficult and time-consuming to make, the work of scribal elites, literate members of the upper class who served—that is, wrote— mainly at the pleasure of the political elites. The Essenes, whose headquarters at Qumran was found to have the long tables, ink, and inkwells used by scribes for copying scrolls, would have been an exception. The members of the sect were, it appears, largely literate; they're believed to have written the Dead Sea Scrolls. But, given that they lived as a small desert community delib- erately apart from the goings-on in Jerusalem, they cannot be thought to have had patrons among the political elite. They worked for themselves, and wrote at the pleasure of absolutely no one. As for your typical peasant family, it's important to remem- ber what we've seen before, and which anthropologist Gerhard Lenski has summed up nicely: "The great majority of the political elite sought to use the energies of the peasantry to the full, while depriving them of all but the basic necessities of life." Bibles, we should assume, would not have been considered necessary.

Although individual sects like the Essenes, and more famously and influentially, the Sadducees and Pharisees, did exist, most Jews would not have aligned themselves with any particular "denomination," in a word familiar to Christians, or branch, the tree metaphor most often used to describe Jewish affiliation today—either Reform, Conservative, or Orthodox, to name just the largest limbs.[5] When considering those everyday reminders of God, there's no need to think a first-century Jew

---

5. Although, call them what you want, branches or limbs, either way, even in modern Judaism, at the center is still a big, fat, ancient trunk.

would find himself in the crossfire of contentious religious debates day in, day out, carried on between members of competing sects while he wandered through the market in Sepphoris or gathered up his nets at the dock in Capernaum.

Of course, various groups did form—with Christians joining the Pharisees, Sadducees, and Essenes, by mid-century. Levine, in fact, starts his description of "religious ambience" by saying that any "[d]iscussion of Jewish religious life in the first century usually revolves around the different sects, most of which were based in Jerusalem." There are two things to note about this. First, Levine is less interested in the theological differences between these groups than in their functions and influence in Jerusalem; once again, except for identifying the Sadducees as the group with the most power, he's just not willing to make definitive statements about who was who or what was what.[6] In one particularly inscrutable moment, Levine notes: "Pharisees might well have been both scribes and members of a *havurah* (religious association) or, alternately, one or the other, or neither. In a similar fashion, we have evidence of poor and wealthy Pharisees, some who were merchants, artisans, or farmers, and

---

6. One key difference between the two most prominent Jewish groups was that Pharisees seemed to believe in an afterlife, whereas the Sadducees did not—a belief that would have had little impact on anyone's daily life. And also, the brutal Pharisee named Saul (later known as Saint Paul) notwithstanding, Sadducees were more inclined to persecute Christians (Goodblatt, "Agrippa I and Palestinian Judaism in the First Century," 9, 15). Nevertheless, for evidence of the Pharisee Saul's hatred of early Christians, consider Acts 8:3: "Saul raided the gathering, going house to house, dragging men and women off to prison," or Acts 9:1–19, where Saul is known for "snorting even greater threats of murder against the Lord's followers" (translated by Wills, *What Paul Meant*, 30–33, 100).

others who were priests, including one presumably high-ranking Temple official."

The other thing to note about Levine's first thoughts on Jewish religious life is that he makes it perfectly clear that just like Jesus, the earliest Christians were no less Jewish than the Sadducees, Pharisees, or Essenes.[7] It may be true that "friction from within and persecution from without" would help move "early Christianity beyond its Jewish and Jerusalem boundaries"—something Levine takes from the New Testament—but as with other Jews, "[d]aily prayer, regular visits to the Temple, and common meals constituted the basis of [Christians'] communal activity." Indeed, Levine concludes, "the Jerusalem church adopted many practices and beliefs that were also normative among the Essenes, including common property, baptism, common meals, and a distinctly eschatological orientation."[8]

Outside Jerusalem, in the hinterlands of Galilee, where Jesus had actually spent most of his time preaching, first-century

7. The earliest Christians were also not likely to have referred to themselves as *Christians*. Not immediately, at least. The meaning of the word *Christ*, Greek for "the Messiah" or "the Anointed," though, was so important to them that, according to Géza Vermes, "within a generation of the crucifixion a Greek neologism, 'Christian,' could be coined in the Judeo-Hellenistic community of Antioch in Syria." But bear in mind that what the earliest Christians identified *the Christ* with was "not just . . . *a* Messiah, but with *the* awaited Messiah of Judaism" (Vermes, 129).

8. Eschatology means, by some definitions, a rejection of the world—its "values and expectations," as Crossan sees it. It looks not to the end of the world per se, but the end of the world as we know it. This was most likely Jesus' version. Others have defined eschatology as a concern with the literal end of the world, the apocalypse or revelation, "immediate divine intervention" (Crossan, *Jesus*, 52–53). This is the version you find in the theology of the *Left Behind* novels, John the Baptist, and often, Saint Paul (Wills, *What Paul Meant*, 100–103).

Christians developed new social and religious practices that would have alienated them somewhat from their neighbors—rethinking the place of women or lepers, say—and a prophetic vision that was perhaps both nostalgic and a little puffed up. In tiny numbers, they thought of themselves as the prophets of old, particularly the northern prophets who likewise had distanced themselves spiritually and geographically from Jerusalem, the center of religious power and, it would seem, corruption. In any case, as Jonathan Reed has said, with rabbis more concerned with "how to negotiate everyday life in the fields, farms, villages, and cities of Galilee," and the everyday people going about their lives in the fields, farms, villages, and cities, the Christians would have hardly raised anyone's eyebrows. Indeed, it seems there was a way to make yourself more marginal as a Galilean peasant in the first century: become a Christian.[9]

---

9. This may, of course, be a chicken-or-egg situation: Did being a Christian make you more marginal, or were the most marginal people simply drawn to the Christians? Crossan, who refers to the followers of Jesus as "hippies" who came up with "a way of looking and dressing, of eating, living, and relating that announced its contempt for honor and shame, for patronage and clientage," believes it was probably both. People have always existed on the margins, and in order to serve the marginal, one had to become marginal (a lesson Dorothy Day, founder of the Catholic Workers, would make relevant in the twentieth century with what she called "voluntary poverty"): "[Jesus'] strategy, implicitly for himself and explicitly for his followers, was the combination of *free healing and common eating*, a religious and economic egalitarianism that negated alike and at once the hierarchical and patronal normalcies of Jewish religion and Roman power" (Crossan, *Jesus*, 198). As usual with Crossan, it's a mouthful. But the ideas make sense. The Jesus movement, as it's often called, took root in a time and place that seemed to call for it. Families were being broken up as landowners were displaced; the numbers of outcasts were on the rise. Poor people were becoming poorer, hungry people hungrier, sick people sicker. And what Jesus said was that they were all blessed because of it. And what would appeal more than joining a movement that not only provided healing and food for everyone, but also taught you to feed and

We mainly know about all these different religious groups
from the first century because they get named in the books
that survived from that time. Sadducees were the most influ-
ential; they had the strongest pull with Rome. And knowing
that Jerusalem was governed by what we would consider today
a religious oligarchy—the spiritual elite known as the High
Priests, surrounded by a legion of Temple priests—we can figure that the Sadducees filled most, if not all, of those positions
over the course of several generations. They were as much the
power players as they were the religious leaders, with all the
attendant complications and concessions involved in being
both powerful and religious. What's more, at regular intervals
throughout the first century, the Romans would remind the
religious elites exactly who was responsible for both their relative religious freedom and their lives of luxury. More than once,
for instance, Rome took hold of both the High Priest's sacred
vestment and what Josephus calls his "long garment," which he
presumably wore underneath. Josephus notes that once, at the
order of the governor of Judea—at this time a Roman named
Fadus—the clothing was locked away in the tower of Antonia,
a fortress near the Temple, so "that it might be under the power
of the Romans." Which basically meant that the very *practice* of
Judaism in the center of the Jewish world was under the power

---

heal? Again, there's no necessary magic behind either feeding someone or inviting a
leper to join you at the table. But for the Jesus movement, both before and after the
crucifixion, healing and feeding would have seemed like miracles all the same.

of the Romans[10]—a fact of which the Sadducees would have needed little reminder.

The Pharisees, who, again, by Levine's account, may or may not have been scribes or members of a religious association, either, or both—well, they're most well known in the Gospels for trying to set traps for Jesus. They ask puzzling legalistic questions and then walk away, having been made to feel like fools after Jesus said things like: "Let any one of you who is sinless be the first to stone her." And debates did go on among these competing religious associations. Those debates are all right there in the Gospels, in Josephus's histories, and in books that collect the sayings of competing schools of first-century rabbis. But what we have to bear in mind is that by and large, an average Jew in first-century Palestine would have stayed out of any high-minded debates and low-punching snipes that characterize so many of the interactions between religious sects in the New Testament, Josephus, or the Talmud.[11] And, we should assume, vice versa.

---

10.   In this case, an appeal to Rome by Agrippa II, the last king of the Herodian dynasty, was met with not just kindness and compliments to the king, but a repetition of the Empire's official line with regard to other peoples' religions. The emperor Claudius wrote: "I have complied with your desire [to have the holy vestments returned] in the first place out of regard to that piety which I profess, and because I would have everyone worship God according to the laws of their own country" (Josephus, *The Antiquities of the Jews* 20.1).

11.   This also means that typical Jews would have remained in the dark about those first-century people and ideas that would, in time, create the Western world as we know it. Religious historian Karen Armstrong and journalist Robert Wright believe that God was making great leaps in his moral evolution during the first century—through the lives of those people who tend to shape our understanding of year one: Jesus and Saint Paul, most notably, and for Wright and Armstrong, the Greek-speaking Jewish philosopher Philo of Alexandria (Wright, 216–41; Armstrong, 68–71). (This is the same Philo of Alexandria whom we've seen say that "women are selfish, excessively jealous, skillful

That is, when it comes to religion as it was really and truly lived and things were really and truly believed, the people who seem to have been in charge were probably a little out of touch.[12]

With that in mind, let's return to the level of brass tacks, where there was no getting around religion in year one because the people we're talking about lived in what they believed was a uniquely holy place. We've seen already that a holiness that covered the whole world erupted geyser-like from its very center[13]—the Holy of Holies at the core of the Jerusalem Temple—and spread itself out thinner and thinner, you might say, the further you got from the source.[14] At least throughout Palestine, God was constantly

---

in ensnaring the morals of a spouse and seducing him by endless charms." Philo's own moral progress appears to have gone only so far.) Still, though Greek language, and with it some Greek culture, had begun to make its way through Palestine—remember, the New Testament was written in Greek—most people would never have heard of this far-flung Jew named Philo. Indeed, we should suppose that, just as with the Roman military presence, within certain, particularly agricultural, communities the real historic weight of Philo's Greek philosophical approach to Judaism would never have been directly felt. Nor, for much of the century (and even longer, really), would *most people* give much thought to preachers like Jesus or Saint Paul.

12. This has often been said about the relationship between American Catholics today and the religious authority of—surprise, surprise—Rome. Take, for instance, some advice writer Paúl Elie offered his fellow American Catholics following the accession of the current pope, Benedict XVI, in 2005: "[W]e ought to turn away from the question of what the pope believes and consider just what it is that we believe— turning our attention away from Rome at long last and back to the world in which the real religious dramas of our time are taking place" (Elie, 92). In other words, according to Elie, the pope just doesn't get it.

13. It should come as no surprise, then—speaking of nourishment emanating from the center of something—that Jerusalem was also talked about as the world's bellybutton (*omphalos*), which, I guess, qualifies Jews of the time as ancient navel-gazers, or, in the words of graphic novelist Glenn Eichler, a bunch of "omphaloskeptics" (Eichler, July 5, 2009).

14. Just for the record, the long and the short of it, according to what's known as Oral Torah, or the Mishnah, puts it this way, which makes holiness seem less, I suppose,

underfoot. Constantly overhead, even. Although one doesn't get the sense that what this meant for a typical Jew was a looming paranoia so much as a feeling of gratitude and, well, inevitability. It was simply the way things were. What came from the ground, what lived in the trees, every hair on your head, belonged to God. And in some ways, most importantly, he was the central piece of history itself. As far as you were concerned, your God was the very same God of your ancestors, and the most essential pieces of what you believed were also the things your ancestors had always believed. Despite whatever natural disagreements might develop over this detail or that within any number of different first-century lives—and once again, argument itself may always have been at the core of Jewish identity[15]—what everyone shared was known in the Greek of the time as *ta patria*. This usually gets translated as "the ancestral things," something they believed, in today's terms, was literally passed down through their genes. For someone living in first-century Palestine, life itself meant to live as your ancestors had, even in your own time.

According to the historian Morton Smith, the ancestors had

---

like an ever-flowing geyser and more like an architectural schematic drawn by the hand of God: "There are ten degrees of holiness. The Land of Israel is holier than any other land. . . . The walled cities (of the Land of Israel) are more holy. . . . Within the wall (of Jerusalem) is yet more holy. . . . The Temple Mount is even more holy. . . . The *hel* is more holy. . . . The Court of Women is even holier. . . . The Court of Israelites is more holy. . . . The Court of Priests is more holy. . . . Between the *ulam* (outer porch of the Temple) and the altar is more holy. . . . The *hekhal* is yet holier. . . . The Holy of Holies is more holy than all of them, for only the High Priests on Yom Kippur at the time of the 'Avodah service can enter therein" (Mishnah *Kelim* 1, 6–9; quoted in Levine, *Jerusalem*, 246–47).

15. Cf chapter II, footnote 8.

always believed, in the words of the third-century BCE High Priest, Simon the Just, that "the world stands on three things—the Torah, the service, and loving acts of kindness." So, as much as possible, you made those things the foundation of your life, as well. After all, if the whole world stood on those things—and in your eyes, since it always had—shouldn't you stand on those things, as well?

What we can safely imagine for those living in year one is daily prayer, probably when they awoke, around noon, and again before they went to bed. They would have faced Jerusalem, considered the center of the world because God himself was said to live there. If they happened to be in Jerusalem, during the Passover pilgrimage, say, they would turn toward the Temple.[16] If they were in the Temple, they would turn toward the Holy of Holies, or, as we've heard before, the very shoe box of God. To prepare themselves for prayer, they may have wrapped themselves in prayer shawls, and, more likely among the elite, wore what are known as *tefillin*, little leather cases that held passages from Exodus and Deuteronomy. What they said in their prayer, whether aloud or in silence, mechanically or with all their hearts, would have contained a profession of faith. Imagining a whole lot more, though, about the individual prayer life of a first-century Jew pushes the limits of decency, as far as I'm concerned. Private prayer, we might as well just assume, should remain a private matter. (For what it's worth, Jesus would have agreed.[17])

---

16. More on pilgrims later.

17. As Garry Wills translates: "When you pray, be not like the pretenders, who prefer to pray in the synagogues and in public squares, in the sight of others. In truth I tell

In public, though, the people would gather at the synagogue. Not every city had one, of course—Nazareth and Capernaum show no evidence from the first century—but where they existed, they became centers of community life. (And where synagogues didn't exist, we can assume people would have gathered in a house.) Jerusalem probably had five, run over the generations by families of priests. And you might expect that residents of tiny villages would make the journey to a nearby city for religious holidays. Sabbath and festival services would have focused on a reading of the Torah and a sermon,[18] and they seemed not to include any communal prayer. Once again, it seems prayer was a private matter, or something shared among friends and family within the home. Hard to call something a "house of worship" when there wasn't exactly what we'd call *worshipping* going on there.

And yet, synagogues mainly operated as community centers. A place where Jews could go not only for Torah and the service (a word that also suggested their commitment to the Temple), but also where they could act out the loving-kindness piece of *ta patria*. The buildings served as soup kitchens and town halls, hostels and even schools. The people came and fed

---

you, that is all the profit they will have. But you, when you pray, go into your inner room and, locking your door, pray there to your Father, who is in hiding, and he, seeing you in hiding, will heed you" (translated by Wills, *What the Gospels Meant*, 86). The house we saw in Capernaum, with its courtyard, the locking door, and several inner apartments, would have suited this sort of prayer just fine.

18. Children—perhaps even girls—would have been instructed in Torah at home, as well (Zolty, 115). But we should assume it was almost always done from memory, perhaps even a rehash of what was covered at the synagogue.

one another, taught one another. The place bustled all week. A visitor always knew he'd have a place to stay. And the Sabbath was hardly more important than the rest of the week. This tradition had been passed down through their genes. And despite all their disagreements and debates, even despite the power of Rome and the culture of Greece, they always had that. Tradition. And the synagogue was the place to practice it.

Arguably the most renowned rabbi of the first century—except, perhaps, for Jesus—was a teacher named Hillel, who, like Simon the Just, famously distilled all of Judaism into only few words: "What you would hate, don't do to someone else: that is the entire Torah, the rest is commentary, go and learn it."

Now, I've said a lot in this chapter about first-century Judaism. I've written a lot of sentences. And to be honest, I think I'd be remiss if I went the whole chapter without acknowledging that this single sentence from Hillel might tell us as much about religion in year one as I could ever do.

IX

WAR IN YEAR ONE

Love your enemies.

—MATTHEW 5:44

For much of the first half of the first century, Roman Palestine seemed quiet. Cities went up. Fields were planted. Many people were fed. Many others were not.

Before it was quiet, though, there was a war—or perhaps *revolt* is the better word. There were a few of them, in fact. Recall that when Herod the Great died in 4 BCE, Rome fended off all comers, "pretenders to the throne," as Josephus puts it, including the bandit chief Judas and his small army in Sepphoris, a city that, after the revolt, was supposedly burned to the ground.[1]

---

1. However, see chapter I, footnote 11.

(And though it remains a mystery precisely what happened to Judas, the simplest way to put it would be that *Rome happened to him*.[2]) A similar thing happened in Peraea, the region to the east of the Jordan River, where a royal slave named Simon apparently "considered that his good looks and great stature entitled him to set a crown on his own head." With a band of robbers, Simon burned down a palace in Jericho, located across the Jordan, and then torched and plundered country estates until the inevitable happened. The Roman infantry attacked, quickly overpowering the uprising. Simon fled up a ravine, maneuvering to avoid a blow from the Roman commander Gratus, and broke his neck. And finally, Josephus reports, there was a shepherd named Athrongaeus who thought he would claim Herod's throne by sheer force of will. What he also had going for him was "his physical strength and contempt of death" and the help of four like-minded brothers. For some time (Josephus isn't clear on this), the five brothers, with Athrongaeus already wearing a crown of his own devising, went around on raids throughout the countryside of Judea, at one point surrounding a hundred Roman soldiers in an effort to cut off the supply line to some 5,000 other men. That same Roman commander Gratus, who ostensibly killed Simon, broke up this attack, but not before the brothers killed the leader of the hundred soldiers—a centurion named Arius—and forty of his best troops.

---

2. We'll see in the following chapter that the Romans, renowned for their orderliness as rulers of an ever-growing number of subjects, were predictably orderly when it came to dispatching their enemies.

The way Josephus describes the state of affairs following Herod's death suggests that Jewish resistance to Rome wasn't particularly well considered, well organized, or well executed. What we know for certain is that when it rose up, rebellion was always bloody and hardly ever actually unified. From this point and for the next seventy-five years, the people who rose up against the power of Rome would be known as brigands, bandits, and robbers. And people like this Judas[3] and Simon would ultimately have less direct impact on Rome than they would on their fellow Jews. And what Josephus writes about Athrongaeus and his brothers eliminates any sense that he was a robber of the Robin Hood variety: "not even a Jew could escape if he fell into their hands with anything valuable."[4]

On the one hand, the activity of these bandits, even as they represented resistance to Roman domination, made travel during the first century quite dangerous. When people moved

---

3. I say "this Judas" because there will be two other, more important Judases to come, one you've probably heard of, named Iscariot, the guy responsible for handing Jesus over to the Romans, and another, also from Galilee, who may have been more responsible than any other single person for the destruction of Jerusalem.

4. Here's a good place to mention that there were, as you might imagine, a good number of pro-Roman Jews out there for bandits to choose from, if they were at once truly rebellious and also discriminating in their tastes of whom to attack and intimidate. (That discrimination is up for debate.) When he met with me to talk about the war in 66 CE, archaeologist Lee Levine compared the breakdown between rebel Jews and pro-Roman Jews to what we saw in America during the years leading up to, and including, the Revolution. There were the "Americans" or "Revolutionaries" (also called "Whigs," "Rebels," etc.), who supported American independence, just as there were the "Loyalists" or "Tories," who believed the colonies should remain a part of the British Empire. These lines were, for the most part, clearly drawn. Although, as Levine finally suggested, we shouldn't forget, in either case—66 or 1776—about the "block of people who just didn't give a damn. They just wanted to live their lives peacefully" (Levine, personal interview, March 20, 2009).

about—say, for religious festivals or to an urban marketplace—
they carried staffs or clubs for defense;[5] when they could they
traveled in caravans or other large groups of families and friends.
They may even have hired guards. And yet, as Rome and its
collaborators applied more and more pressure from the top and
wandering bandits threatened from below—that is, when things
got really, really bad—individuals were often forced into banditry
themselves.[6] An ancient example of *If you can't beat 'em, join 'em.*

This is the argument made by J. D. Crossan, whom we've previously seen make the claim that women and girls who threatened the financial stability of the home by not getting married
young enough might be forced into prostitution. He says something very similar about the men and boys who became bandits
when presenting a family with a comparable threat: "It is necessary neither to romanticize nor canonize them but to understand that their increasing presence always indicates that the

---

5. Knowing this makes Jesus' command to his itinerant followers not to carry a staff
seem at once foolish and risky as well as of a piece with an approach to the religious life
that, while certainly resisting Roman power, seems to have advocated nonviolence.
It might also be worth pointing out that when you have thirteen men hanging out
together, it's best not to go around looking too much like armed robbers. That said, for
this very reason, J. D. Crossan considers it "unthinkable" that Jesus and his disciples
would have all traveled together from place to place throughout Galilee. "Imagine,"
he says (as usual), "that group arriving in a hamlet with all the men out working in
the fields and only women and small children at home, especially in an honor-and-
shame culture divided among gender lines. Bandits!" (Crossan, *Jesus*, 108–9).

6. The parable of the "good" Samaritan not only helps us understand who hated
whom in year one, but also to see just how dangerous travel could be. Remember,
before the Samaritan could be "good," a traveler had to be beaten: "Once a man was
going from Jerusalem to Jericho, and he encountered thieves, and they tore his clothes
off and beat him, and went away leaving him nearly a corpse" (Luke 10:30; translated
by Wills, *What the Gospels Meant*, 130–31).

oppressed lower classes are being pushed below even subsistence level and are being forced into armed resistance, however sporadic, ineffective, or desperate." What prostitution and banditry seem to have had in common was desperation. And if we're to believe what Josephus says about some of the bandits he writes about, desperation could force you into stealing from your own people. We shouldn't doubt this possibility; after all, we've seen it before. What's the difference between bandits stealing a traveler's wealth and wealthy Sepphorians, with Rome's help, buying up the land from peasants just so those peasants could pay brand-new taxes on land they'd owned for years. And let's also not forget that after they sold the land they often continued working it, as either indentured servants or tenant farmers.

This was the experience on the ground, so to speak, the desperation that increasingly led people to resist Roman rule through unrestrained violence. And knowing what's to come— that is, the full-blown war that would begin in 66 CE—Crossan once again asks us to visualize what we cannot see. "Imagine peasant resistance like a giant iceberg. Most of it is covert, hidden below the surface, and not visible at all to the elites against which it is carefully aimed." This also means that most of the rebellion was not visible to the elites writing the histories, especially those writing from a distance and often years after the resistance and wars were over. I'm not willing to say that much of the peasant struggle was aimed all that carefully. But it's finally safe to say that Tacitus, who lived and wrote in Rome, was wrong. All was not quiet.

Despite the various disorganized and often amorphous

groups resisting Roman rule (some by robbing anyone and looting anything they could get their hands on), many of them shared a common ancestry, so to speak, in a religious sect formed by another rebel named Judas, also from Galilee;[7] his movement, a direct response to the more hands-on Roman rule and increased taxation that began in 6 CE, was known as "the fourth philosophy," essentially because it would come to be considered a branch of Judaism right alongside the Sadducees, Pharisees, and Essenes.[8]

Judas the Galilean is remembered as an early militant leader whose entire career in summed up in a single verse of the Acts of the Apostles, where he's named by a Pharisee named Gamaliel

---

7. While I consider this Judas to be a different Judas than the one mentioned above, it's not impossible that they were actually the same person. Even so, I'll remind you that what we saw way back in chapter I's very long footnote 10 suggested they were not.

8. You may have noticed that this "fourth" status is similar to the one we gave to Christianity in the previous chapter, where by mid-century the movement that Paul inherited was just gaining ground as an alternative to the three other most widely recognized "branches" of Judaism. (An alternative that most people would have ignored, just as they did the other three.) It's even been argued that Judas the Galilean and Jesus of Nazareth were actually the same person; Daniel Unterbrink lists thirty-three similarities (an auspicious number, of course, given how long Jesus is believed to have lived) between the two, and even calculates the odds at 262,000 to 1 "that Jesus and Judas were separate individuals" (Unterbrink, 201). Of course, much, much more survives from the first century in terms of what's been written about Jesus, and as we've shown, most scholars are still unsure about exactly who this Judas the Galilean actually was. (Some others doubt that Jesus ever even existed.) But Unterbrink's creating odds like that makes me think that he protests too much and actually reminds me a little of what certain Christians today have to say about, of all things, premarital sex. To borrow again from Jeff Sharlet, by some accounts, he notes, "men who have sex before marriage are something like 600 percent more likely to experience a drop-off of sexual passion once they are married." Which means that after doing the math, Sharlet reckons "the incentive for premarital chastity is stunning: a post-wedding life of sex that's 600 percent more awesome" (Sharlet, June 23, 2005).

as one in a short list of dissidents who stood up in opposition not only to paying taxes to Rome, but also to Jewish collaboration with the Empire: "Judas the Galilean rose up at the time of the census[9] and got people to follow him; he also perished, and all who followed him were scattered." This is all we ever hear of Judas in the New Testament. And what Gamaliel, clearly a Jewish collaborator with Rome, is attempting to do by mentioning Judas is to remind those gathered what happens to people who oppose the Empire. They die. And his message, of course, was to include Jesus and his followers: "So in the present case, I tell you, keep away from these men and let them alone; because if this plan or this undertaking is of human origin, it will fail; but if it is of God, you will not be able to overthrow them—in this case you may even be fighting against God!" The meaning is clear; as far as a wealthy elite like Gamaliel could tell, God and Caesar had somehow ended up on the same side. Josephus himself would come to argue the very same thing: "What corner of the earth had escaped the Romans," he writes, "unless heat or cold made it of no value to them? From every side fortune had passed to them, and God, who handed dominion over from nation to nation around the world, abode now in Italy." Yet, for the likes of Judas the Galilean (and we can also imagine Jesus of Nazareth), God would never leave Jerusalem; and in words now usually associated with the first tenet, or pillar, of Islam,

---

9. This census would have been used to create what were essentially tax schedules regulating who owed how much to Rome.

Judas rebelled against Caesar because there is no god but God. Believing this got him killed.

And yet, by most accounts, the bandits and robbers and guerrilla fighters that slowly but surely rose up over the next sixty years in the cause of political independence were all "Judas's spiritual heirs." No matter where they were scattered, they took root in some form. Some of them we'd consider "common thugs and general criminals," as Crossan and Reed have noted; still others we would recognize as "liberators" and "freedom fighters,"[10] scrambling through the hill country and fighting piecemeal what the Romans considered a *bellum servile*, or "slaves' war." Rome believed the more respectable way to fight was head on, with armies marching out against them—a *bellum justum*, as it was known; that is, a "just war," or more accurately, as Crossan and Reed say, a "real war." Fighting bandits and terrorists was, to the Romans, like fighting lowly slaves. It was a new, unconventional war with a new name—not so different, I suppose, from what nowadays we've alternately called the "Global War on Terror" and "Overseas Contingency Operation." The question is what you call a "war" when there aren't traditional "soldiers" fighting on the other side. As you see, it's an age-old problem.

There were also some notable examples of nonviolent resistance against Rome—including what have been called "martyrological protests." For some Jews death would have seemed

---

10. This is something we acknowledged as far back as the Introduction, footnote 5.

better than any alternative. In one instance dating to 26–27 CE, by order of the Roman prefect Pilate, troops set up images of Caesar within the walls of Jerusalem; in direct response, some protesters gathered in Caesarea, where Pilate was then stationed, and "fell prone all round his house and remained motionless for five days and nights," as Josephus tells it. On the sixth day, Roman troops surrounded them and Pilate threatened "that he would cut them to pieces unless they accepted the images." As you might expect, the Jews refused to budge, and "as though by agreement fell to the ground in a body and bent their necks, shouting that they were ready to be killed rather than transgress the Law." Pilate relented. And this public-relations disaster—a show of weakness by Rome—that crisscrossed the country might explain once and for all why Pilate chose to locate a Roman-style construction project like the Tiberium in the outwardly pro-Roman Caesarea. Lesson learned.

A similar incident dating to the early 40s challenged Rome with more than public-relations trouble; nonviolent resistance amounted to an agricultural strike in Galilee. From the Jews' perspective, the problem was the same: Petronius, a Roman deputy from Syria, wanted to install graven images in Tiberias. And the Jewish response was what you'd expect: "The Jews replied," reports Josephus, "if he wished to set up the images in their midst, he must first sacrifice the whole Jewish race: they were ready to offer themselves as victims with their wives and children." The standoff would last some fifty days, and Petronius realized that "the land was in danger of remaining unsown." By 40 CE, this represented a real problem in Galilee, where, we've seen, "corn was king." And knowing this, Petronius sent himself packing and put those tenants back to work in the fields.

The varieties of effective resistance to Rome—from guerrilla warfare to an agricultural strike—were in constant flux throughout the century. The Gospels themselves are a single, if inconsistent, account of an impressive, yet small, Jewish peasant movement against the power of Rome. (Just think back to Jesus calling Herod Antipas "that fox"; remember his advice to give back to Caesar what is Caesar's; recall how fearful he seems to have been of setting foot in Sepphoris.) And while Josephus fills his book about the war with story after story of Jews mustering the courage to fight back, we can assume he's accounting for only the most obvious forms of protest. There's no record, say, of tiny gatherings of devout Jews praying for God to step in and treat Rome the way he'd treated Egypt when he sent all those plagues and drown Israel's enemies in the Red Sea. And yet, it's not hard to imagine just this sort of prayerful protest. (Nor should it be hard to imagine those people believing their prayers would come true.) There are some—Crossan and Reed, for example—who would argue that the most powerful Jewish resistance of all involved no show of arms, no claims to religious authority, and no prayers for an "immediate divine intervention." For them, resisting the power of Rome meant simply being Jewish—that is, simply being pure. In this way, *miqwaoth* and chalk measuring cups were weapons anyone could wield. Indeed, as we've seen, everyone did. As the authors conclude, "Jewish purity is about Jewish identity, about fundamental Jewish resistance to Greco-Roman submersion, and about the future: that is, whether there will be a future, for the Jewish tradition, the Jewish people, and the Jewish God."

There was, of course, no first-century version of the Red Sea in the long-standing Jewish fight against the Romans. God appears to have stayed out of it. And all the stone vessels and ritual baths in the world weren't going to hold back an empire that would rule over lands stretching from Britannia to Mesopotamia—that is, from England to Iraq. So, while we can assume that nonviolent resistance continued in pockets throughout Roman Palestine, that people persisted in prayer, and that bands of brigands carried on in robbing and killing the wealthy—those whom Josephus calls "respectable citizens"—if the Jews were going to stand any chance, their resistance to Caesar would have to, in a sense, coalesce.

By mid-century, two particular groups would begin to emerge with ambitions to more deliberately and more effectively make some noise in Roman Palestine. They gained special influence as the actual rebellion took shape in 66, a time when, as even Tacitus would have admitted, the land was anything but quiet. They were, like Judas the Galilean and his scattered followers, proud and violent nationalists known respectively as the Sicarii and the Zealots.

The Sicarii began to operate in a concerted way in Judea sometime in the 50s,[11] forming what we might call urban

---

11. This is what Josephus says, in any case. Although, we might assume they'd been working, perhaps less concertedly, for decades. Jesus himself seems to have made friends with one: Judas "Iscariot," whose name probably derives from his work as a political assassin (Wilson, 128–29).

terrorist cells.[12] They were named for the short daggers they hid beneath their cloaks, known in Latin as *sicae*. "Their favorite trick," writes Josephus, "was to mingle with festival crowds, concealing under their garments small daggers with which they stabbed their opponents. When their victims fell, the assassins melted into the indignant crowd, and through their plausibility entirely defied detection." Not only skilled assassins, the Sicarii were also, it seems, Oscar-worthy actors. Their first victim was the High Priest himself, Jonathan, who had his throat slit. Not surprisingly, since the High Priests and their Temple priests were more obviously political appointments than religious ones—and they were as often in contact with Rome as they were with God—these leaders were often targeted by the Sicarii; although, so was anyone with ties to the Empire. And after Jonathan fell, "many were murdered every day."

By 66, the Sicarii had grown relentlessly confident in their ability to terrorize the aristocrats and religious elites of Jerusalem, if not also the population at large. "More terrible than the crimes themselves," says Josephus, "was the fear they aroused." Their first actual leader was a man named Menahem,

---

12. In an age obsessed with terrorism, it should come as no surprise that the word has a contemporary usage, as well, referring to hit men at the center of the Mexican drug trade; they're called the *sicarios*. Says one former Mexican assassin, "I have no idea how and when I became a *sicario*. At first, I picked up people and handed them over to killers. And then my arm began to grow because I strangled people. I could earn $20,000 a killing. . . . *Sicarios* are not born, they are made" (Bowden, 47). Of course the same could be said of the original Sicarii; only in their case, it wasn't drug cartels but the Empire that made them.

the grandson (probably) of Judas the Galilean.[13] Judas's "fourth philosophy," in fact, has been identified specifically with the Sicarii; Lee Levine actually equates them: "the Fourth Philosophy (or Sicarii)." What this tells us is that, in a sense, in Roman Palestine urban terrorism became a viable alternative in the religious universe that included the piety of the Essenes, the Roman collaboration of the Sadducees, and the annoying legalese of the Pharisees. Under Menahem's command, the Sicarii would gain control of Masada, a mountainous fortress and Roman stronghold on the Dead Sea. They would fight the war from there—essentially holed up.

The second group to consolidate—perhaps loosely—in opposition to Rome seems to have done so with the express purpose of fighting a war. The Zealots, who have often been confused with the Sicarii (even by Josephus),[14] were probably

---

13. Josephus calls Menahem "the son of Judas the Galilean," but to me (and others) the timing seems a little off (Josephus, *The Jewish War*, 167, 462). It's not impossible, of course, but given that Judas's revolt took place in 6 CE (which is also when he died), it seems unlikely, especially given life spans back then, that you'd find someone as old as Menahem would have to have been taking leadership of a powerful and violent group of terrorists in 66—Osama bin Laden, 53, notwithstanding (Josephus, *The Jewish War*, 166, 434).

14. Josephus uses the word "Zealot" only once when referring to the followers of Menahem, who in every other case are called Sicarii (Josephus, *The Jewish War*, 167, 462). It was the Sicarii who stationed themselves in the fortress of Masada; it was the Zealots who formed to fight the war in Jerusalem. By Crossan and Reed's account, they were "forced inside the protective walls of Jerusalem as Vespasian's scorched-earth devastation swept southward in the winter/spring of 67–68" (Crossan and Reed, 190–91). This confusion has caused some trouble in certain arguments about Jesus—say, concerning who he was and who his friends were—which is part of the reason why we've kept our consideration of him brief. But, where there's a point to make about history, like when we talked about the "miraculous" tile roof in Capernaum (chapter III), it's worth digging through the mud a little. Now, there's little disagreement about the

made up of the same nationalistic brigands, robbers, and guerrilla fighters we saw earlier. These "crazy men," as Josephus calls
them, were led by a man named Eleazar.

The name Eleazar, like Judas, was a common one among
the revolutionaries, which probably has something to do with
the confusion between the Zealots and the Sicarii. So, just so
we're clear: The Eleazar who led the Zealots was the son of a
man named Simon. There was also an Eleazar who later led
the Sicarii at Masada; the cousin of Menahem, this Eleazar was
the son of a man named Jarius. To add to the confusion, we
have a third Eleazar, son of the High Priest Ananias. And in
Josephus's eyes, it was the actions of this Eleazar, the Temple
captain, that led inexorably to war: "[He] persuaded the minis-
ters of the Temple to accept no gift or offering from a foreigner."
Which meant no sacrifices for Rome or Caesar.

That said, it's probably impossible to identify precisely what
caused the full-bore war that began in 66 and ended in 73 with a
mass suicide of the Sicarii at Masada. We certainly shouldn't try

---

possibility that Judas Iscariot was a Sicarii (see footnote 11 in this chapter): historically, it adds up. On the other hand, the possibility that Simon the Zealot, one of
Jesus' other disciples, was technically the kind of Zealot we hear about in Josephus,
is far-fetched. That's not to say Simon (or Jesus, for that matter) couldn't have shared
ideas or even objectives with the Zealots that fought the war in Jerusalem. But Simon
the Zealot was not, for our purposes in looking at this war, technically a "Zealot."
And when popular historian A. N. Wilson argues that it is of "supreme interest that
Jesus chose a Zealot to be one of his close personal followers" after first noting that the
Zealots, not the Sicarii, had taken control of Masada, well, he makes a mistake that
seems most clearly intended to present us with who Wilson thinks Jesus was (Wilson,
128–29). And it's not impossible that Jesus was friends with violent men. But Wilson
should have stopped with Judas when trying to make that point. The rest gets history
wrong (although, to be fair, so does my guidebook for Israel).

to pinpoint a single cause. Explanations try to place blame—it was the bandits, the Zealots, the Sicarii; the Romans, even the Greeks, who in the late fifties battled with Caesarean Jews over civic rights and control of the city. We've seen economic disparity and families threatened; taxes were continually on the rise. Feeling these particular pressures, at the outset of war the Sicarii set fire to the Record Office in Jerusalem, "eager to destroy the money-lenders' bonds and so make impossible the recovery of debts, in order to secure the support of an army of debtors and enable the poor to rise with impunity against the rich." Some blame even has to fall on an unnamed Roman soldier who, in the spirit of Monty Python, farted in the general direction of a crowd of Jews: "The people had assembled in Jerusalem for the Feast of Unleavened Bread, and the Roman cohort stood on guard over the Temple colonnade, armed men always being on duty at the feasts to forestall any rioting by the vast crowds. One of the soldiers pulled up his garment and bent over indecently, turning his backside towards the Jews and making a noise as indecent as his attitude." The crowds responded by throwing stones. And with an overreaction perhaps unparalleled in all of history, the Romans counter-attacked, crushing, by Josephus's report, some 30,000 people.[15]

Whatever the cause, the war began. It was fought on different fronts throughout Palestine. Most Galileans joined the

---

15. In his later work, *The Antiquities of the Jews*, Josephus lists the numbers of people killed, essentially by this fart, at 20,000. Exaggeration aside, we can be sure that lots of people died (Josephus, *The Antiquities of the Jews* 20.5.3).

side of the revolt, or, as Crossan and Reed speculate, "once hostilities broke out and indiscriminate violent Roman reprisals became certain, Galileans fled to fortified sites for temporary safety." Other Galileans fled to Jerusalem, along with refugees from Peraea and other parts of Judea. After a surprise victory against Cestius Gallus, a Roman deputy from Syria who had quickly conquered much of the land already, the Jews believed victory could be theirs. That optimism would not last long. Nor, in the scheme of things, would their city and its Temple.

The story of the Jewish revolt against Rome, in a sense, begins and ends in Jerusalem. (And it's this city's destruction that accounts for all the finger-pointing over the war. After all, who wants to be responsible for destroying such a marvelous city of God?) For two years, the fighting took place between the insurgents in the city—the Zealots, especially, joined by groups of Idumeans,[16] and rebels led by men named John of Gischala and Simon bar Giora—and an ever shifting Jewish authority. By 69, those early allegiances had fallen apart, and though the Zealots and John had gained control of the Temple, it quickly became less and less clear exactly whose side anyone was on. The city was, by all accounts, in anarchy. And this was before Rome even came to town.

All the while the Romans had been encircling the city—watching it burn, you can imagine. And after a year of waiting while the Empire sorted out who would succeed Nero, who

---

16. Idumea, recall, is where Herod the Great hailed from. (See chapter II.)

died in the summer of 68, as emperor, the final siege began. Beginning in the spring of 70, fighting with battering rams and spear-throwers, catapults and *ballista*,[17] daggers and arrows, the parties met across walls protecting the city. They were fortified by the Jews and knocked down by the Romans, a wall at a time. Piece by piece the inevitable happened. During the reign of Vespasian, Rome leveled the center of the world, burning the Temple, burning the ashes, and then seemingly burning the ashes again.

"I have heard," wrote the Roman historian Tacitus, "that the total number of the besieged, of every age and both sexes, amounted to six hundred thousand. All who were able bore arms, and a number, more than proportionate to the population, had the courage to do so. Men and women showed equal resolution, and life seemed more terrible than death, if they were to be forced to leave their country. Such was this city and nation."

It's been said that "everything appears to promise that it will last." In first-century Palestine, Jerusalem offered this promise more than any other place on earth. And in year 70, the Jews learned the truth, and the end of these sentiments of Benjamin Franklin: "In this world nothing is certain but death and taxes." They'd paid their taxes and then they died. And Tacitus's quiet returned to the land.

Such *was* this city and nation. Past tense.

---

17. Catapults and spear-throwers threw weapons; the *ballista*, a similar machine, threw stones (Josephus, *The Jewish War*, 436).

X

DEATH IN YEAR ONE

Follow me, and leave the dead behind to bury their dead.
—MATTHEW 8:22

If I've said it once I've said it a thousand times: To understand what it was like to live in Jesus' world it does us little good to look directly at him.[1] It's clear that by all accounts Jesus felt the weight of Rome and the pull of money differently than other first-century Galileans. He doesn't appear to have believed in family, work, or study the way other people did. He had what might safely be called an unusual perspective on healing, eating, and drinking. The man didn't feel at home in his hometown and had no political attachments.[2]

---

1. And if you've grown a little tired of my saying this I can't really blame you.
2. "There is no such thing as a 'Christian politics,'" writes Garry Wills. "If it is a politics, it cannot be Christian" (Wills, "Christ Among the Partisans," April 9, 2006).

He hardly recognized the law and baffled even his closest friends with his ideas about war and peace. And perhaps strangest and most dangerous of all, Jesus didn't practice religion like his fellow Jews.

But, while for our purposes any real-life itinerant like Jesus would mainly be a "ragged figure who moves from tree to tree" across these pages, when the moving did eventually stop and he called out in a loud voice, "My God, my God, why have you abandoned me"—well, at his most ragged this man stopped moving from tree to tree and was nailed to one, giving us reason finally to pause and take a look at him.

"Christus," says Tacitus, "suffered the extreme penalty during the reign of Tiberius at the hands of one of our procurators, Pontius Pilatus." While the penalty this second-rate Roman governor issued to a poor artisan from Nazareth may have been extreme, crucifixion was hardly uncommon. In *The Jewish War* alone, Josephus records the deadly crosses of unnamed thousands (though not the cross of Jesus[3]). As always, Josephus exaggerates in terms of the real numbers, but just consider this description of Jerusalem and the handiwork of Florus, procurator of Judea, in the lead-up to the war that began in 66:

---

3. Josephus does, however, mention Jesus, Pilate, and the crucifixion in his history *The Antiquities of the Jews.* But when he wonders whether "it be lawful to call him a man" and then refers to Jesus directly as "the Christ" (or, "the Messiah"), we're left to wonder whether those lines might have been added by a later writer, a member of what Josephus calls "the tribe of Christians . . . [who] are not extinct at this day" (Josephus, *The Antiquities and the Jews,* 18.3.3).

The total number that perished that day, including women and children—for not even infants were spared—came to about 3,600. The disaster was made even more crushing by the unheard-of character of the Roman brutality. No one had ever before dared to do what Florus did then—to scourge men of equestrian rank before the new judgment-seat and nail them to the cross, men who were indeed Jews, but all the same enjoyed Roman status.

Or this, as evidence of just "how loyal the Jews were to each other and how *contemptuous of punishment*": "when a man from Jotapata had been captured he had borne up in the face of the most horrible tortures and even when the enemy used flames to extort information had refused to say a word . . . finally going to death by crucifixion with a smile on his face." With just these two examples in mind, whether exactly 3,600 Jews were killed on a single day or one man from central Galilee was actually smiling all the way to the end, in light of the utter brutality involved in crucifixion, accounting for every detail seems a little beside the point. Ultimately, what it says to us is that while Jesus, the most famous crucified man in history, may not have lived like the people around him, when he died, he died brutally, just like so many others of his day. Maybe even a little faster.[4]

Today, of course, images of this instrument of Roman torture are everywhere. There's little arguing with poet David

---

4. And today, just as in Jesus' own time, one might take some little comfort in the reports that he spent only six hours on the cross. Indeed, we're told the quickness took Pilate by surprise (Mark 15:44).

Berman's[5] quip: "If Christ had died in a hallway we might pray in hallways / or wear little golden hallways around our necks." And of course, I would not be the first to point out that from *Ben-Hur* to *The Life of Brian*, or from Martin Scorsese to Mel Gibson, versions of this "extreme penalty" have played across our movie screens for more than half a century. (And going back even further, Americans have seen burning crosses on film since *The Birth of a Nation*, which is to say the earliest days of Hollywood blockbusters.) Nor has it gone unsaid that similar depictions have appeared in the world of visual arts, recently in a controversial photograph of a tiny plastic Christ submerged in a glass of the artist's urine and the somewhat more appetizing, though no less controversial, 200-pound chocolate sculpture of Jesus created in 2007 by Cosimo Cavallaro. Cross tattoos adorn the back of soccer player David Beckham, the shoulders of Justin Timberlake and NBA star Allen Iverson, the ankle of Drew Barrymore, and the lower backs of both actress Eva Longoria and my younger sister, to name only a few. And to this day Madonna continues her decades-long fascination with the death of Jesus[6]—from her 1980s neckwear to a life-size mirrored cross she hung from during her 2006 *Confessions* world tour.

Once among the greatest forms of torture imaginable, this cross is now (and still) a spectacle, protest, and decoration, all

---

5. Until January 2009, Berman was also the only consistent member of a band he founded in 1989 called Silver Jews who recorded a song called "Rebel Jew," which was at least in part about Jesus' death on the cross.

6. Or—and pardon me for this—to borrow from a 2004 *Daily Show with Jon Stewart* bit about Mel Gibson's *The Passion of the Christ*, I'll call this Madonna's *crucifixation*.

at the same time. And like Jewish prayers, land disputes in Palestine, and even industrial farming, the Roman cross has followed us, in any number of ways, through centuries of new days.[7]

But what made dying on that cross, as Garry Wills reminds us while quoting Cicero, the "extremest penalty" (*summum supplicium*) issued by the Romans—worse than beheading, being gored and eaten by animals in the circus, or being burned alive (in that order)?[8] Though I hate to put too fine a point on torture and will stop just short of asking you to imagine exactly what any of this must have been like,[9] to answer the question requires that I describe as plainly as possible how someone would have died after being fastened in whatever way to a Roman cross.

In more cases than not, the cause of death would have been suffocation. Bound either by ropes or by nails running through the wrists and ankles—feet straddling each side of the center,

---

7. And I suppose, as Berman has said, the same would be true for any Roman hallway that saw the death of Jesus.

8. More of a crank than David Berman, Garry Wills goes on to point out in his book *What Jesus Meant* that "crucifixion involved a whole galaxy of horrors," and then of course wonders "if young people consider that when they wear gold or jeweled crucifixes as earrings or necklace pendants" (Wills, *What Jesus Meant*, 111). *Young people?* Of course some. But I doubt that young people are the ones lining up outside Tiffany and Co. for a $9,300 Jean Schlumberger Maltese Cross of diamonds in 18 karat gold— the smash hit *Gossip Girl* notwithstanding.

9. David Foster Wallace concluded a 2004 essay about animal suffering and the Maine Lobster Festival by saying, "There are limits to what even interested persons can ask of each other" (Wallace, 254). In that spirit, and assuming we're all still interested, I've decided that asking you directly to imagine being tortured, or to imagine yourself torturing someone else, is where I draw that line.

upright beam—the man might hang on the cross for hours, sometimes more than a day. In advance of being nailed to the beams, he may have been scourged, or burned, as in the case of the man from Jotapata, which would have been, in some unbelievable way, a mercy. Already weakened, his time fighting for breath might have been shortened some. (This may have been the case with Jesus, who was reportedly scourged.) Already half-dead, his legs may have been broken after a few hours to speed up the process. (This was not, apparently, the case with Jesus.) In the time a man spent on the cross, his own body weight would gradually become too much for him to lift for breath—even as his shoulders loosened from their sockets and his wrists broke and bled. All that body weight would finally settle on his chest and kill him.[10]

This was the death of Jesus.[11] This was the death of countless men at the hands of Florus and of one loyal Jew from Jotapata. And finally, we know it was also the death of a first-century man named Yehochanan, pulled from his ossuary in northeastern Jerusalem in 1968, the only crucified skeleton ever

---

10. And the death was filled with as much panic as pain, which is another way the effects of the Roman cross have followed us into the current day. In a 2008 *Vanity Fair* article, "Believe Me, It's Torture," journalist and cultural provocateur Christopher Hitchens, who as an experiment underwent the "enhanced interrogation technique" known as waterboarding, describes it not as an experience of "simulated" drowning but of actually being drowned—"annihilatingly" smothered (Hitchens, August 2008). I think of the suffocation involved in crucifixion in similar terms where the panic is concerned. But the whole process of being crucified would have been deeply complicated by the fact that as it's happening the condemned man was actually tearing his own arms from their sockets, and by the other, certainly more troubling fact that the condemned man was, in fact, *condemned*—and he knew it.

11. Is it any wonder the man felt abandoned by his God?

discovered—not just from the first century, and not just from Palestine, but the first and only *ever*. And there is a reason why, in all the time spent combing this part of the world for bones and stones and potsherds, archaeologists have found only one crucified skeleton. That reason, in large part, involves dogs.

Yehochanan, crucified in his mid- to late twenties, was lucky to be buried—and for no other reason than that part of the punishment of crucifixion was to know your dead body would not be buried, and would, in all likelihood, be devoured by animals. In that way, we're lucky he was buried, too. After all, his skeleton, which was carefully studied by both Israel's Department of Antiquities and Jerusalem's Hadassah Medical School, gives us our first tangible evidence of how someone might have died on a cross. J. D. Crossan has imagined for us the gory details:

> [Yehochanan's] arms had not been nailed but tied to the bar of the cross, probably with arms to elbows over and behind it. His legs had been placed on either side of the upright beam, with separate nails holding the heelbone [*sic*] to the wood on each side. A small olive-wood plaque had been set between the nail's head and the heel bone lest the condemned man manage to tear his foot free from the nail.

The damage had been done, his torture complete, Yehochanan's death was final. And yet, when archaeologists took his body from where it had lain for centuries, pieces of the cross were left behind, preserved, petrified, twisted and knotty and now actually part of the body after all these years. Crossan concludes: "But the nail in the right heel had struck a knot in the upright and its point had become bent, so that when the man was taken down, the nail, the olive wood, and heel bone all remained fixed together in burial and discovery."

We're lucky to have Yehochanan's preserved skeleton because it tells us what life might have been like for a last few moments in first-century Palestine. And again, what makes this particular condemned man luckier than, say, all those others Josephus tells us about is that his body was never subject to the ultimate humiliation or, for the family and friends he left behind, the all-consuming horror, of becoming food for wild animals.

I first learned of the fate of most crucified men while reading Crossan's *Jesus: A Revolutionary Biography*. In that book the author quotes a German scholar named Martin Hengel, whose book *Crucifixion in the Ancient World and the Folly of the Message of the Cross* highlights the humiliation and degradation involved in being crucified, including the aftermath, which usually meant, in Hengel's words, serving "as food for wild beasts and birds of prey." Hengel and Crossan both look back to ancient writings that detail this horrifying relationship between man and animal: the condemned were "fastened [and] nailed . . . [as] evil food for birds of prey and grim pickings for dogs," executioners "feed the crows on the cross," and those who suffered on the Roman crosses "hung . . . alive for the wild beasts and birds of prey."

Finally, though, what Hengel and Crossan help us see is that crucifixion was not meant just as torture but also as terror, in which even the animals played an important role. (One might also grimly suggest that offering up the dead as food for wild dogs played a small part in making them man's best friend.[12]) Watching bodies, naked bodies, first die and then slowly be consumed over time—an arm dropping off, a leg hanging low—would have been an appalling warning against rebellion. This would have been especially true among the devout lower classes, a hotbed of rebels and terrorists and the source of the revolt that was so completely annihilated by the Romans. Josephus describes the public aspect of crucifixion as a fate worse than death, a fear the Romans would take every opportunity to exploit: "It happened that in this battle one of the Jews was taken alive. Titus ordered him crucified before the walls, hoping that the sight would terrify the rest into surrender." And as if this single man nailed to a cross in the typical arms-out-legs-straight manner wasn't humiliating or terrifying enough, Josephus offers countless naked and twisted bodies as a warning of the complete and absolute "doom closing in on the City." From the sidelines, Titus, the emperor's second in command, would chalk up an overflow of bodies to the interest of national security and the tactical disadvantage involved in employing so many troops as prison guards. For the

---

12. Henri Daniel-Rops, who scoured the Bible creating his portrait of first-century Palestine, adds: "As for the dog, which is mentioned more than forty times in the Bible, it was not the friendly inmate of the home as it is in the West but a half-wild animal, with some mixture of jackal or wolf, thin from want of food and ill-natured, which roamed the streets and performed the office of scavenger by eating carrion and filth" (Daniel-Rops, 28). And from what I can tell, if the varieties of mangy dogs wandering around Bethlehem today are any indication, nature has yet to completely take her course.

commander, it was not just easier to kill everyone he rounded up, but exceedingly more effectual. And for Titus's soldiers, crucifixion was just a lot more fun.[13]

> Titus indeed realized the horror of what was happening, for every day five hundred—sometimes even more—fell into his hands. However it was not safe to let captured men go free, and to guard such a host of prisoners would tie up a great proportion of his troops. But his chief reason for not stopping the slaughter was the hope that the sight of it would perhaps induce the Jews to surrender in order to avoid the same fate. The soldiers themselves through rage and bitterness nailed up their victims in various attitudes[14] as a grim joke, till owing to the vast numbers there was no room for the crosses, and no crosses for the bodies.

From the death of a man once hailed by a few Romans, in a grim joke, as the "King of the Jews,"[15] and the deaths of countless like him, we'll turn now to the death of an actual Jewish king selected by the entire Roman senate, whose end was

---

13. For more Roman fun, think of Jesus' crown of thorns, his royal purple cloak, and the mock salute by the soldiers assigned to him, "Hail, King of the Jews" (John 19:1–3). This amounted to what Garry Wills calls a "burlesque of a coronation" and "an improvised game" (Wills, *What Jesus Meant*, 110). And this is hardly any fun at all when compared with what Josephus will describe.

14. A different translation makes clearer what is meant by "various attitudes": "The soldiers out of rage and hatred amused themselves by nailing their prisoners in different postures" (quoted in Crossan, *Jesus*, 126). What I think we're getting at here is feet-where-the-head-should-be, or hands-together-feet-together-lengthwise, or heads-to-shoulders-knees-and-toes, and everything in between.

15. This was also the crime he was famously charged with.

marked not only with a gruesome and painful illness and some dramatic efforts to revive him, but also, as Josephus describes it, "a virtual challenge to death itself." If death was opening the doors for Herod the Great, he would clog the passage with more bodies than death could handle—beginning with a couple of rabbis.

When Herod was almost seventy—"old and despondent," as Josephus puts it—he grew deathly ill.[16] The earliest days of his "distemper" were consumed with settling old and new scores and amending his will so that his son Antipas would gain control over Galilee.[17] (We know how that turned out.) But things would very soon get much, much worse for King Herod—to say nothing of what was about to befall two men who took this moment to test the king with a popular uprising. Believing they were striking "a blow for God," two rabbis named Judas and Matthias put it into the heads of their students to go up and tear down the golden eagle the king had situated above the Great Gate of the Temple. Apparently this

---

16. While they certainly might apply, in this case let's just forget about those distinctions we made earlier between illness and disease and between healing and curing. The king was dying. No ifs, ands, or buts. (For the discussion of healing vs. curing, and the differences between illness and disease—borrowed from Crossan's *The Birth of Christianity*, 293–98—see chapter VI, footnote 16.)

17. Other amendments included giving 1,000 talents, roughly sixty million times a tenant farmer's daily wage (Josephus, *The Jewish War*, 466), to the emperor, and half that to his wife and his family, Caesar's friends, and his freed slaves; what was left, including Herod's land, was divvied up among his other sons and his sister Salome, whom he made "very rich, because she had continued faithful to him in all his circumstances, and was never rash as to do him any harm" (Josephus, *The Antiquities of the Jews* 17.6.147–48). (Salmone, incidentally, had had a hand in plotting Herod's murder of his beloved wife Mariamme.)

blow was best struck in broad daylight: "At mid-day," reports Josephus, "when masses of people were walking about the Temple courts, they lowered themselves by stout ropes from the roof and began to cut down the golden eagles with axes." This would not last long. Seized almost immediately by Herod's troops, about forty young men in total were gathered up and brought to the ailing king. "Forgetting his sickness," in typical King Herod fashion the king "exploded with rage." Convinced by the gathered crowds that only a small number were really guilty, the king did, however, express some leniency. Only "those who had lowered themselves from the roof together with the rabbis he burnt alive." The rest he turned over to his attendants for execution.

Next up for Herod, though, was the "mortification of the genitals, producing worms." Suddenly remembering his illness, his whole body gave way, which some blamed on what he did to Matthias, Judas, and their followers:

> [T]he sickness spread . . . accompanied by a variety of painful symptoms. He had a slight fever, an unbearable itching all over his body, constant pains in the lower bowels, swellings on the feet as in dropsy, inflammation of the abdomen . . . as well as difficulty in breathing, especially in lying down, and spasms in all his limbs.

And yet still, King Herod wasn't done. Worried over exactly the sort of meager funeral he might be given—especially after his latest outrages against his own people—Herod locked up "the most eminent men of every village in the whole of Judea"[18] and left his sister Salome and her husband with these orders: "as soon as I die, kill them all." His funeral, he decided, would have to piggyback on theirs.

And yet, only half of what Herod told his sister would come to pass. After further attempts to treat him with hot baths and hot oils failed, after once attempting to kill himself with his apple knife, and after a few more executions under his belt, King Herod finally expired. All those prisoners were let go.

King Herod's rule lasted thirty-six years. He died just before Passover, 4 BCE. And like that, we're back where we started.

But before moving on and wrapping up, it's worth asking what exactly killed King Herod. What made him so spectacularly sick? As we might suspect, speculations abound—everything from gonorrhea ("in view of his many marriages") and arteriosclerosis to chronic renal failure and Fourier's gangrene. In 2005, though, a London surgeon named Houman Ashrafian pointed out what all those theories seem to overlook—the symptom that, to both the untrained and the ancient eye, seems most obvious: HEROD'S GENITALS WERE CRAWLING WITH WORMS, or what the doctor calls "ectoparasites."

In a letter to the editor of the *Journal of Infection*, the diagnosis Ashrafian offers, with an appropriate touch of good

---

18. Given this example of Herod's homicidal insanity, a recent threat to kill all the newborns in Bethlehem doesn't seem at all unlikely.

humor,[19] is scabies, or the Itch—*Sarcoptes scabiei* var. *hominis*. Ashrafian figures this invasion of tiny eight-legged mites was complicated in Herod by a strep infection, which would have accounted for his terrible stomach problems. The doctor concludes:

> The adult female mites are approximately 0.4 mm long and males 0.2 mm, which are on occasion visible to the naked eye. These would also have been seen 2000 years ago, as it is unlikely for human visual acuity to change in this period. It would be highly unfair, therefore, to assume that our ancient colleagues were unable to precisely inspect a pathological state such as infestation with visible ectoparasites by simply denying their observations as inaccurate.

And so went King Herod the Great. Ravaged by an infestation of worms, each no longer than half a millimeter.

If we agree that crucifixion was, as Josephus described it, "the most pitiable of deaths," and that Herod the Great kicked it in a way that was truly spectacular, what can we say about a first-century death that was less pitiable, one that was more typical than either Jesus', Yehochanan's, or Herod's? Was any

---

19. E.g., "If we are, however, to apply the fundamental adage of hoof prints implicating horses more than zebras (except in Southern Africa!) . . ."

death back then really run-of-the-mill? Or, can we just agree that, then as now, from the perspective of the dying man or woman, no death is truly unspectacular? After all, each death has its own effect on the life of the dying and on the life of anyone who's ever lived to watch someone die—something first-century Jews felt as intensely as they felt their own souls. After all, who doesn't want to be remembered?

In year one, what being remembered involved was, above all, a proper burial—something not afforded to a man picked apart by scavenging dogs after he died on a cross, or, as Herod feared, a king who believed his death would be celebrated with "wild rejoicings." Indeed, according to Martin Hengel, "What it meant for a man in antiquity to be refused burial, and the dishonour which went with it, can hardly be appreciated by modern man." And as you might imagine, Herod's fear of dishonor in this case, unlike a man nailed to a cross, was totally unwarranted. The king's burial could not have been more magnificent: "There was a solid gold bier, adorned with precious stones and draped in the richest purple. On it lay the body wrapped in crimson, with a diadem resting on the head and above that a golden crown, and the sceptre by the right hand." Followed by a parade of soldiers, Herod's body was escorted more than twenty miles by his sons and other family, and then buried at Herodium, just as he had commanded.[20]

---

20. After a thirty-five-year search, Israeli archaeologist Ehud Netzer located Herod's grave on the northeastern slope of Herodium in 2007, claims supported by new excavations of the site in late 2008 (Kraft, May 9, 2007; Hebrew University of Jerusalem, November 30, 2008).

Still, the promise of a burial, even a far less elaborate one, would have been just as important to an everyman Jew as it was for the Jewish king. And as with most rituals in Jewish life, the roots of the practice can be found in the Bible, where the prophet Jeremiah describes the humiliation of going unburied, bodies left on the land as food for birds and dogs, and the inconsolable family who cannot mourn. Jeremiah later warns that the burial of an unworthy king will be like the burial of an ass, "dragged off and thrown out beyond the gates of Jerusalem"— that is, he will have no burial at all.[21] From Genesis to Deuteronomy to Ecclesiastes and beyond, Jews worth their salt were given the proper burial—from carpenters to kings.

In some ways, what remains from typical first-century burials is just what we'd expect and tells us much of what we already know about the importance of family in Jewish life—and, yes, Jewish death, as well—and also reveals more about how matters of purity distinguished Jews from the rest of the world.

Yet, before getting too specific, one thing we can learn, in general, from tombs around Palestine is contained in the burial inscriptions themselves and requires a little math. According to J. D. Crossan, "Judging from extant burial inscriptions, the life expectancy of Jewish males in the Jewish state was then twenty-nine years." That is, more often than not, life in Jesus' time ended before you were thirty. And so, for all their uniqueness, both Jesus and Yehochanan were, statistically at least, pretty normal guys.

---

21. It's no wonder Herod was so nervous.

Yehochanan, Crossan tells us, was buried with his family—indeed, generations of his family—in an ossuary. This single stone box, filled with the bones of thirty-five people,[22] was contained within a burial complex among fourteen other ossuaries, arranged in four different tombs, which had been dug out like four separate rooms into the limestone at a site called Giv'at ha-Mivtar. In the tombs there were also hollows large enough to hold single bodies, which would be buried there as soon as possible after death, although never on the Sabbath. When the body had decomposed it would receive a second burial, which for most Jews—especially among the wealthy, like Yehochanan—would be within an ossuary of the kind where he and his family were found.[23]

And though we know that even some peasants were able to afford ossuaries, or, in other cases, buried their own dead *again* in dug-out shafts, we still have to assume a great deal about the classes of people absolutely unable to afford these stone boxes for burial. As if we needed more evidence that we'll always know more about the ones who could afford to be remembered,

---

22. Crossan tells us how the others in that ossuary had met their end, which gives us a good sense of the variety of different ways your average Jew, young and old alike, might have met her end in the first century: "Of those thirty-five, one woman and her infant had died together in childbirth for lack of a midwife's help; three children, one of six to eight months, one of three to four years, and another of seven to eight years, had died of starvation; and five individuals had met violent deaths: a female and a male by burning, a female by a macelike blow, a child of three to four years by an arrow wound," and, last but not least, Yehochanan, by crucifixion (Crossan, *Jesus*, 125).

23. As you might expect, you'd find the same kind of burials—that is, typically Jewish—throughout Jesus' Galilee, as well (Reed, 50).

for those who couldn't, all their dried-up bones are lost to the sands and stones of Palestine.

About even those lost bones, though, we can be sure of one thing: When they were buried, they were buried outside the cities, villages, and hamlets where people gathered. (And from what we know, they may only have been buried once, in a shallow grave.) Cemeteries belonged in the wilderness, beyond the walls, because a corpse was an impure thing. Even Jesus'. He was crucified at Golgotha, the "place of the skull," outside Jerusalem, and was anointed with oils, and then buried in a garden nearby, in a brand-new tomb. A dead body, he was kept away from the living.

WE'VE NEARLY REACHED THE END OF OUR JOURNEY

Jesus was born in Bethlehem of Judea in the days of
King Herod.

—MATTHEW 2:1

Today, people traveling to Bethlehem, a tiny strip of a town in the West Bank, arrive from Jerusalem, which sits about six miles to the north. And as pilgrimage destinations go, Jerusalem has always been something of a big brother to the little town identified in the Gospels as the birthplace of Jesus. As with most older siblings, Jerusalem has had a decidedly rougher go of it over time—the Western Wall, all that remains of the city's once great Temple, is a clear reminder of that. And the X-ray machine, metal detectors, and armed soldiers at the entrance to the site are all the evidence you need that the city's history may get rougher still. But a quick consideration of those grow-ing pains—to say nothing of the growing pains of Jerusalem's pilgrims—might, in fact, tell us something about how we both imagine and ultimately see Bethlehem, its inhabitants, and the pilgrims who flock there today.

As we know, ancient Jewish writers often idealized what's known today as the Old City. For them, it was the world's most sacred metropolis, the seat of the Temple. And as they imagined it, from upon the Temple Mount to within the Temple walls everything got holier still as you approached the mysterious, indescribable, and basically off-limits Holy of Holies, the dwell-ing place of God. (Think back to the passage about Israel's ten degrees of holiness I quoted earlier.) Jerusalem, with its Temple, was essentially the center of the universe, the very navel, as it was known, of the world. That is, the whole world was believed to be nurtured by this dazzling city—a city Jews from everywhere supposedly nurtured in turn with annual tithing. And every year at Passover Jews from throughout the known world flooded Jeru-salem for what they imagined would be the feast of a lifetime.

Jerusalem's destruction in 70 CE was related to what Jose-phus referred to as this "huge influx from the country." While not pilgrims exactly, the Jewish nationalists that most strongly opposed the Romans—first, the terrorists known as Sicarii, and then the religious Zealots, both parties of brutal killers—found their strongest support among those who, like them, had most idealized Jerusalem and so most hated those who had come to rule over them with implicit (and occasionally explicit) threats to defile their land and its most holy city. But if we're thinking about pilgrims, we can, for the most part, probably assume that ideal-izing Jerusalem is not specifically—or perhaps not at all—a war-time mentality.[1] It's also not simply an ancient way of thinking. Instead, it may simply be something the pilgrim's mind does.

With that in mind, what if we were to imagine again the people living during those years between 14 and 37 CE, when Tacitus mis-takenly believed that "all was quiet" in Palestine? That's exactly what I asked archaeologist Lee Levine to do when I visited him in Jerusalem in early 2009.[2] Curious what Levine thought of those far-flung Jewish peasants we met very early in this book, people he stopped just short of calling "country bumpkins," I asked what someone from first-century Galilee might have thought about Jerusalem.[3] As we might suspect, someone with Jesus' background,

---

1. Although even today we'd probably find considerable overlap between those with highly romantic notions about Jerusalem and those most willing to fight—even con-trary to Israeli law—to defend every Jewish settlement in Gaza or the West Bank.

2. Lee Levine's work, if you haven't noticed, shows up more than once in the end-notes to various chapters of this book. His name appears again in the Acknowledg-ments, in large part because he warned me very early on, and with characteristic good humor, about trying to answer any specific question concerning daily life in first-century Palestine: "Let me make a general statement," he said, looking at some notes and research questions I'd written for the book. "Most of the things that I see there, I don't know the answer. . . . And I would even be a little arrogant and say that no one knows the answer."

3. Full disclosure: I was, in fact, thinking about Jesus when I asked this question. I had in mind a scenario proposed by J. D. Crossan in his biography of Jesus. Giving his take on the moment when Jesus overturned the moneychangers' tables and cast them out of the Temple, Crossan writes:

> I am not sure that poor Galilean peasants went up and down regularly to the Temple feasts. I think it quite possible that Jesus went to Jerusalem only once and that the spiritual and economic egalitarianism he preached in Galilee exploded in indignation at the Temple as the seat and symbol of all that was nonegalitarian, patronal, and even oppressive on both the religious and the political level. Jesus' symbolic destruction simply actualized what he had already said in his teachings, effected in

he said, "probably had a very romanticized, beautiful image of the Temple and purity and sanctity and drama," and when he arrived in Jerusalem as a pilgrim, he would have found that "it can be a messy place." There's no denying it, Levine continued: "You have animals here, money; probably people argued about how much. . . . I can't imagine there isn't [haggling] when you're dealing with money and buying." So, finding moneychangers at the Temple, "He"—that is, Jesus—"was turned off!"

Then, taking a moment to think, Levine, an American who resettled in Jerusalem in the late seventies, continued: "I think most Jews who have never been to Israel—they come here and they see that with . . . all the achievements of Israel . . . there's [still] a problem with driving, there's a problem of politeness, of getting on a bus and waiting your turn." In other words, what travelers even today often fail to imagine, perhaps even as they're packing their bags, is the very thing ancient pilgrims might also have failed to understand—which hints at just how similar today's Old City might actually be to ancient Jerusalem. Then and now, you're sure to find the sacred and astonishing right there alongside the profane and ordinary.

---

his healings, and realized in his mission of open commensality. But the confined and tinderbox atmosphere of the Temple at Passover, especially under Pilate, was not the same as the atmosphere in the rural reaches of Galilee . . . and the soldiers moved in immediately to arrest him. (Crossan, *Jesus*, 133).

Basically, Crossan is saying that, like any Jewish peasant of his day, Jesus probably romanticized the Temple and, finding it far less *perfect* than he'd imagined and far less *perfect* than he preached, he threw a fit. That fit, in turn, led to his arrest, and ultimately his crucifixion. Far less inclined to dabble in such "historical reconstructions," as Crossan puts it, when I asked, Levine would not speculate on what might have led to Jesus' arrest, or just how often he'd been to the Temple, or really much of anything at all.

With these final words, Levine confirmed for me something I proposed at the outset. That, along with so many of our other attitudes and behaviors—from our simple desires to stay clean and well groomed to our most complicated fears about death and dying—when we consider our power of imagination, there is nothing deeply and essentially different between who we are now and who we were then. Yes, the very same kind of romanticizing goes on even today, and an age-old problem resurfaces. As Levine concluded during our conversation, when someone is treated impolitely or simply has to wait in line for a bus,[4] "all of a sudden this romantic picture becomes blurred." Which may mean, in simple terms, that sometimes the pilgrim just can't see straight.[5]

To get to Bethlehem, we begin, as I've said, about six miles away. These might be six of the longest miles in a pilgrim's life. And for what it's worth, the way back is even longer.

---

4. Although waiting outside my hotel those fifteen minutes for the bus to Levine's house was slightly annoying, and during my ride I witnessed no fewer than three displays of impoliteness, for his part the driver did make sure I got off the bus at the right stop and, as if being rewarded for looking out for me, was presented with both an apple and a cucumber by an old man apparently heading home from the produce market, who in addition to the produce also paid the driver his full 6.80NIS fare, no questions asked.

5. And since I'd like to conclude this book with my integrity intact, if not exactly with what we might all agree are a few clear-eyed observations about Bethlehem, this problem with seeing straight makes me ask, once again, in the words of Flannery O'Connor: "Does one's integrity ever lie in what he is not able to do?" I find O'Connor's answer as helpful now as it was when we began: "I think that usually it does" (O'Connor, 5).

In Jerusalem, groups of Christian tourists climb aboard chartered buses and arrive in the heart of Bethlehem, Manger Square, after first visiting Rachel's tomb,[6] just on the outskirts of town. Pilgrims traveling alone or in smaller groups pile into a Sherut, a short bus about half the length of a Greyhound, which makes local stops along the way. Or travelers hail taxis, which, if bound for Bethlehem, are all driven by Palestinians—as are the Sheruts. Today, and since the 1949 armistice, Bethlehem is in Palestinian territory, and the average Israeli is not allowed into the town. Which accounts for about half the reason this trip is so much stranger than you'd expect.

I was even told what to expect.[7] A military checkpoint with long—even humiliating—lines. A twenty-six-foot-tall East Berlin-style barrier wall. Yet, when the bus reached its last stop and deposited us on the side of the road, so far we'd encountered no armed soldiers and no passport control. Instead, we met a jovial

---

6. This is the biblical Rachel who died giving birth to her son Benjamin. Her husband (and first cousin) Jacob is believed to have buried Rachel on this spot on their way to Bethlehem, marking it with a pillar of eleven stones. Jacob, the Jewish Patriarch, was the father of the twelve tribes of Israel. (Israel, in fact, is the name he was given just before Rachel died.) The eleven stones of Rachel's tomb mark the eleven sons alive when she died—Benjamin would be the twelfth. As for Rachel, she was Jacob's second and favorite (and, well, *concurrent*) wife, whom he married after being tricked into marrying Leah, Rachel's sister (Genesis 35; Genesis 29:15–30). Incidentally, Jacob also famously wrestled with an angel (perhaps the archangel Michael) (Genesis 32:22–31). Today, Rachel's tomb is highly fortified and sits behind a security wall to separate it from Bethlehem. We're talking armed soldiers, barbed wire, and a guard tower. Israeli pilgrims take bulletproof buses.

7. Just to clear up any confusion that may result from referring to myself both in the singular (I, me) and in the plural (we, us), I'll add here that I was accompanied throughout my travels in Israel and Palestine by someone who goes nameless here but whom you'll find properly thanked in the Acknowledgments.

cabbie named Ahkmed in an idling taxi. He said that for a set price it would be "no problem"[8] to take us where we needed to go. He knew the town as well as anyone because he'd grown up there. Probably in his late forties—and I say probably on account of some language issues, owing mainly to my complete ignorance of even polite Arabic—he had friends and family there. He would introduce us to some of them, who all had other friends or relatives in New York. In words used by the international public relations campaign called Open Bethlehem,[9] Ahkmed is a Bethlehemite.

Driving around Bethlehem must be as hard on a car as driving around San Francisco. It's all hills and tight fits, plus white limestone. No one goes fast, which makes for a good tour. So, on what we still thought was our trip to the checkpoint, Ahkmed drove by the best of Bethlehem's political art, pointing out walls covered in the characteristic stencil paintings of renowned British graffiti artist Bansky: a dove in a bulletproof vest caught in the crosshairs of a sniper rifle, a girl in a pink dress patting down

8. For Ahkmed almost nothing was a problem. While his English was infinitely better than my Arabic, part of the initial confusion about my actually being *in* Bethlehem at this point, despite not having crossed through a checkpoint, can be chalked up to my sense that his English was actually quite good, and that when I said I wanted to go into Bethlehem (a town, it's worth repeating, *I was already in*), and that to get there I wanted to pass through the checkpoint, I figured he understood what I meant. Instead he said, "No problem," which, it eventually became clear, was what he said to anything he didn't understand.

9. The campaign, launched in 2005 to highlight Bethlehem as a "living example of an open and multi-faith Middle East," claims the support of former U.S. president Jimmy Carter and South African archbishop Desmond Tutu, who has noted, "Open Bethlehem is a nonviolent attempt to save a city that belongs to many in the world. It is unconscionable that Bethlehem should be allowed to die slowly from strangulation." More on what Tutu refers to as the "strangulation" of Bethlehem to come.

a soldier. Bound for the Christian pilgrimage sites, we'd of course already begun the tour. For Ahkmed, the inside of the security wall that surrounds Bethlehem is just as worth seeing—as much a pilgrimage site—as the cave beneath the Church of the Nativity where Jesus is said to have been born. The wall speaks for itself, telling a story about a great event. This land and its people have been divided, and it's very clear that there's enough blame to go around.[10] Including some for me.

The words covering the wall and buildings throughout the town are mainly in English. A gate large enough for tour buses to pass through is decorated with a painting of a U.S. dollar and scrawled with the words "escape hatch." Individual sections of the wall have been stenciled with the phrase: "MADE IN U.S.A." And one of the most striking paintings, which stretches across six individual sections of the wall and nearly reaches over the top, is the iconic image of boxer Sugar Ray Robinson raging at Jake LaMotta, Robert De Niro's "Raging Bull." Even after seeing all this, I still didn't know I'd reached my destination. So far I'd thought I'd been looking at the outside of the wall.

That quickly changed. Strolling alongside Ahkmed down Milk Grotto Street toward Manger Square—and by down I mean *down*; Bethlehem, like so much of Palestine, is a puzzle of hills—my new friend told me that crowds (which are modest

---

10. This is not, of course, the place to try to offer explanations, solutions, or really even opinions about the Israeli-Palestinian conflict. It is, however, a place to acknowledge that it's almost impossible to ignore its impact on the people of Bethlehem, who are increasingly unemployed and whose major revenue source—that is, tourists like me—has dropped off precipitously since the wall went up in November 2005.

these days) reach their heights, and he does his best business, at Christmastime, which might have gone without saying, I suppose. Christians flock to Bethlehem for Christmas, just as during Dhu al-Hijjah, the twelfth month of the Islamic year, at least once in their lives Muslims like Ahkmed journey to Mecca, in Saudi Arabia, shouting, "Here I am, O Lord, I am here!" as they approach the city.[11]

The Christian sites of Bethlehem are, of course, unmistakable: Milk Grotto Chapel, a solemn, beautiful little church known for its rocky interior, believed to have changed from red to white when some of Mary's milk dripped onto the stone while she was feeding Jesus; St. Catherine's Church, a plain Franciscan cloister that dates back to the Crusades; and of course, the Church of the Nativity, a building commissioned by Constantine in 326, which today is decorated with not just candles, an ornate crucifix, gilt Eastern Orthodox icons, and, in places, a fourth-century mosaic floor, but also a flurry of massive silver lamps hanging from the rafters and strung with convenience-store Christmas ornaments. And if, as I've said, all the security around Bethlehem accounts for one half of what made my visit stranger than I'd expected, the scene at the Church of the Nativity accounted for the other half.

Arriving through Manger Square, pilgrims bow to pass

---

11. The object of a Muslim pilgrim, or a *hajji*—since the annual pilgrimage itself is known as the *hajj*—is the Kaba, the cube-shaped House of God containing a sacred black stone believed to have been given to Ibrahim (the biblical Abraham) by the angel Gabriel as a sign of God's covenant, through Ibrahim's son Ismail, with the Muslim community. Muslims believe that Ibrahim and Ismail built the Kaba and that it was the object of pilgrimages even in pre-Islamic times (Esposito, 91–92).

through the church's tiny Door of Humility before crowding down some steps into the grotto where it's believed Jesus was born. The spot is marked on the floor with a fourteen-pointed silver star, and pilgrim after pilgrim—tourist after tourist— bends down to touch and often kiss the holy ground; others rub a Bible wrapped in a plastic bag over the star, hoping, it would seem, to take home with them a little bit of the site's holiness.[12] Even so, from any number of vantages, what's most prominently on display in the grotto of the church is a collection of pilgrim bottoms. It was impossible to get a clear look at the star with so many backsides in the way.

For whatever reason, Ahkmed waited outside the Christian sites for us. He said it was no problem. And mainly because I was so slow to understand that I had actually maneuvered legally between Israel and the West Bank, it took me some time really to feel comfortable around him, which I'll blame for my one small but lasting regret about my time in Bethlehem.

---

12. Similar things happen at Jerusalem's Church of the Holy Sepulchre—visitors bowing low, kissing and rubbing the marble stone that covers the rock on which Jesus' body was supposedly laid to rest. In this church we see the same attempts to take away some of the magic, both through contact with the stone and an endless series of flashbulbs—proof, I suppose, that the pilgrim has made the trip. The scene at the Western Wall, however, feels quite different, much less about taking something away than giving something back. The plaza you reach after passing through security is divided into a courtyard for men and a courtyard for women. Most notable about the men, whose heads are all covered, is their constant rocking, twisting, and bowing during prayer—a process called "davening." Most notable about the women, so I was told, was that many of them didn't stop crying the whole time we were there.

After leaving the Milk Grotto, Ahkmed led us down toward Manger Square and into what he claimed was the oldest olive wood factory in Bethlehem (which, by the looks of it, may very well have been the case). Though constructed of the same limestone that makes Bethlehem—like most everywhere else in the Holy Land—glow with the changing color of the sun at dawn, then noon, then dusk, once inside it felt as though this building had been dug from the earth. Three workmen sat carving olive wood with small power tools; they made piles of amulets and trinkets in the shapes of the Virgin Mary, a cross, hearts, and leaves. These, it seemed, were sold up and down Milk Grotto Street. And from inside the shop Ahkmed took us up to the uneven roof of the building, where in the distance he pointed out the flat-topped Herodian, site of Herod's tomb, an ancient fortress built by the king that was described by Josephus at its height as "having the shape of a women's breast."[13] As we left, continuing down the street past any number of other small wood-carving factories, Ahkmed invited us for tea. A friend owns a shop around the corner, he seemed to be saying. It would only be a few shekels. Were we thirsty?

I said no. No, we weren't thirsty.

---

13. It's also known as Herodium. And Josephus goes on:

> [Herod] encircled the top with round towers, filling the enclosed space with a palace so magnificent that in addition to the splendid appearance of the interior of the apartments the outer walls, copings, and roofs had wealth lavished upon them without stint. At very heavy cost he brought in an unlimited supply of water from a distance, and furnished the ascent with 200 steps of the whitest marble; the mound was of considerable height, though entirely artificial. Round the base he built other royal apartments to accommodate his furniture and his friends, so that in its completeness the stronghold was a town, in its compactness a palace (Josephus, *The Jewish War*, 83).

"No problem," Ahkmed said once again, leading us on to the Church of the Nativity. And right then I knew we'd missed our chance.[14] And the sad fact was, after a few hours of travel, we were thirsty. Tea would have been perfect.

The Israeli army is there to greet you after you leave Bethlehem on your way back to Jerusalem, a city recently described to me as a "magnetic mess." At that moment, as our short bus pulls over to the side of the road, the whole country feels like that; the pilgrim is drawn here; everything is so attractive—the histories, the religions, the stories, the people. But they're all in such disarray, just as they were two thousand years ago.[15]

At the checkpoint, you file out of the Sherut with the locals, and a soldier checks your passport before allowing you back into the bus. Truly: no problem. Everyone seems fairly used to it. Among the Israeli guards, Americans seem to get special

---

14. In journalist Peter Manseau's experience on Turkey's Revelation Road—a path that connects seven cities mentioned in the book of Revelation—two schoolteachers he encounters, Ulas and Gokcen, pose a similar question. Only Manseau, a better traveler than I, knows how to answer the question correctly. More experienced pilgrims say yes. He recalls:

> Ulas covers her face to stifle more laughter, but Gokcen forges ahead. "Do you like to drink something? Liquids? Soft drinks or tea?"
> "Do I like drinking liquids?" I ask. There's nothing like travel to cause you to answer questions you never thought to consider. "Yes, I do like drinking liquids," I say, "when I am thirsty."
> "We would drink anything with you." (Manseau, September 14, 2008)

I would drink nothing with Ahkmed.

15. Shall we count the ways?

treatment.[16] Smiles, for one thing. And more tellingly, a mere glance at the passport. And back on the bus—no questions asked.[17] But still, it's hard to ignore that those Israeli soldiers have huge guns. And they sure seem young.

Travel like this—and also of the strange, historical kind we've done in these pages—should challenge us. On the one hand, it dares us to see things clearly, to look at the stories that have brought us here, and realize what our imaginations have done to the world we live in. Believe what you will about what took place in Bethlehem or throughout Palestine some 2,000 years ago. But make no mistake: the Holy Land today is not all heavenly hosts and blessed pilgrims. We are impolite and messy people; we carry guns and shove our way into the little corner of a room where we've been told Jesus was born. We build walls and blow up buildings. We don't trust an American writing a history book or an Arab taxi driver who offers us tea. And we've always been this way.

---

16. The same cannot be said about passport control at the airport in Tel Aviv. Questions abound. Which leads me to offer this suggestion to travelers: If possible, avoid telling Israeli passport controllers you are writing a book. Because if you say you're writing a book, officials of increasing size and severity will interrogate you, make phone calls about you, grimace to each other in an obvious way, ask you to please have a seat in the other room, make you wait while they discuss you in low (and, to your ears, foreign) tones, then question you again about any intentions you have to visit the West Bank (which, yes, you do, since that's where Bethlehem is), then talk about you again in increasingly serious tones, take phone numbers of the archaeologist you'll be interviewing in Jerusalem, etc., all the while you—to say nothing of your poor traveling companion who had no trouble at all with her passport official—nervously begin to wonder whether honesty is always the best policy.

17. Although I was told by one of the soldiers, who appeared to be showing off for his friends, not to be a fag.

But we're also another way. We give a bus driver a piece of fruit and offer directions in our best approximation of whatever pidgin language we need; we honor the sacrifices of our soldiers and prepare little corners of tiny homes—in New York City and Bethlehem alike—for new children. We paint our protests on some walls and have been known to raze other walls to the ground. We build new buildings and invite complete strangers into our homes. We write new stories, volunteer in our communities, and offer a pilgrim a cup of tea. And as we know, we've always been this way, too.

Imagine that.

ACKNOWLEDGMENTS

I would like to thank my editor, Jake Morrissey, for making this book possible; thanks, as well, to Megan Lynch for introducing us. Additional thanks to Sarah Bowlin, Elizabeth Wagner, and the rest of the hardworking folks at Riverhead.

Jim Rutman is a supremely thoughtful and generous agent. He is lucky to have the support of a wonderful assistant, Adelaide Wainwright. Thanks to both.

Many thanks to Patrick Stayer for his translations. Jerusalem-based archaeologist Lee Levine provided not only his expertise about life in year one but also important and humbling advice with regards to writing about it. Thanks to Chanan Tigay for introducing us. Sarah Stodola and Kira Brunner Don from *Lapham's Quarterly* were kind readers of pieces of an early draft.

Student researchers did much of the heavy lifting for this book. Special thanks to Simon Geballe, Zara Khaleeli, and Shana Oppenheim for their essential contributions. Natalie Zutter saved me from the embarrassment that would have come from facts going unchecked. I am grateful, as well, for the professional support of June Foley, the Writing Program Director at New York University's Gallatin School of Individualized Study.

Special thanks to my family. Frank, my brother, was an early reader. Countless friends offered regular and much-needed encouragement. Thanks, in particular, to Peter and Amy Bebergal, Sara Burningham and George Hamilton, Elizabeth Little and Dylan Kidd, Jennifer Murray, and Taly Ravid. Additional special thanks to M. Ryan Purdy.

Ahkmed, the Bethlehemite we meet in the Epilogue, was the best guide to his hometown I could have hoped for. My one nagging regret about this book is that I didn't stop with him for tea.

Finally, Kate Garrick went along with me on this journey into year one. My profoundest thanks go to her—for every day, every mile, every page.

NOTES

Translator's Note: On the Epigraphs for *Life in Year One*

Page(s)

2   *"Blessed are they which do . . ."* Matthew 4:25.

Author's Note: On Writing *Life in Year One*

Page(s)

7   *"O mortal . . ."* Ezekiel 3:1.

Introduction: This Is Not a Book About Jesus

Page(s)

11   *This war has come down . . .* Josephus, *The Jewish War,* translated
        by G. A. Williamson, revised and edited by E. Mary Smallwood
        (London: Penguin, 1970), 27, 473–74.

11   *It has not gone without saying . . .* E. Mary Smallwood, "Introduction,"
        in Josephus, *Jewish War,* 13.

12   *Philo wasn't particularly concerned . . .* David E. Aune, *The New
        Testament in Its Literary Environment* (Philadelphia: Westminster
        Press, 1987), 42.

13   *"All the prisoners taken . . ."* Josephus, *Jewish War,* 371.

13   *a city whose entire population . . .* J. D. Crossan, *The Birth of
        Christianity* (New York: HarperOne, 1998), 417; Lee Levine,
        Jerusalem: Portrait of the City in the Second Temple Period
        (Philadelphia: Jewish Publication Society, 2002), 340–43.

15   *"If Jesus is a mere man . . ."* Quoted in Garry Wills, *What Jesus Meant* (New York: Viking Penguin, 2006), xvii–xviii.

16   *"That belief in Christ . . ."* Flannery O'Connor, "Author's Note to the Second Edition," *Wise Blood* (New York: Noonday, 1962), 5.

16   *"it must be assumed . . ."* Helmut Koester, *Introduction to the New Testament, Vol. 2: History and Literature of Early Christianity* (New York: Walter de Gruyter, 1982), 73–74.

16   *"[h]e was an illiterate peasant . . ."* J. D. Crossan, *Jesus: A Revolutionary Biography* (New York: HarperOne, 1994), xii, 58.

17   *"seated among the scholars . . ."* Luke 2:46–47; translated by Garry Wills, *What the Gospels Meant* (New York: Viking Penguin, 2008), 123.

17   *"At first he says nothing . . ."* Wills, *What the Gospels Meant*, 180–82.

17   *"Let any one of you . . ."* John 8:7; translated by Wills, *What the Gospels Meant*, 181.

17   *"wrote nothing for his followers . . ."* Wills, *What Jesus Meant*, xix.

        "We are not told . . ." Wills, *What the Gospels Meant*, 181.

18   *"pidgin language"* . . . Wills, *What Jesus Meant*, xi.

19   *It was a practical Greek . . .* Eugene Peterson, *Eat This Book: A Conversation in the Art of Spiritual Reading* (Grand Rapids, Mich.: Wm. B. Eerdmans, 2006), 142–43.

20   *"words are strung together . . ."* Wills, *What Jesus Meant*, xi.

20   *what we know as "biblical English"* . . . Ibid., xi–xii.

21   *"[apostle] was not an office . . ."* Garry Wills, *What Paul Meant* (New York: Viking Penguin, 2006), 189–90.

21   *And what has been translated* . . . Ibid., 180–81.

21   *"rough-hewn majesty . . ."* Wills, *What Jesus Meant*, xiii.

22   *"Imagine the standard Mediterranean family . . ."* Crossan, *Jesus*, 59–60.

22   *"When one looks at the level . . ."* Christopher Moroney, *Ancient Echoes: Music from the Time of Jesus and Jerusalem's Second Temple* (Franklin Park, Ill.: World Library Publications, 2003), 3.

22   *"tiny hamlet of Lower Galilee,"* where we can suppose . . . Crossan, *Jesus*, 26, 194; Jonathan L. Reed, *Archaeology and the Galilean Jesus* (Harrisburg, Pa.: Trinity Press International, 2000), 83.

"the highest level of professional . . ." Moroney, 3.

Anything we say about . . . A. N. Wilson, *Jesus: A Life* (New York: W. W. Norton, 1992), xiii.

I. The World in Year One

Page(s)

26   *First to be captured* . . . Josephus, *Jewish War*, 74.

27   *and by all accounts incomparable* . . . Ibid., 81.

27   *"Herod went to Bethlehem . . ."* Matthew 2:16; translated by Raymond Brown, quoted in Wills, *What the Gospels Meant*, 71.

27   *Herod is said to have* . . . Henri Daniel-Rops, *Daily Life in Palestine at the Time of Christ* (London: Weidenfeld and Nicolson, 1962), 459.

30   *"the common people . . ."* Tacitus, *Histories* 5.13.

30   Population figures for Nazareth and Capernaum drawn from Reed, 83, 152.

32   *"All was quiet"* . . . Tacitus, *Histories* 5.9; quoted in Crossan, *Birth of Christianity*, 9.

33   *In the tumult that followed* . . . Reed, 100; Josephus, *Jewish War*, 126–27.

34   *a Greek title that loosely means "prince"* . . . E. Mary Smallwood, "Glossary of Technical Terms," in Josephus, *Jewish War*, 495.

34   *Building a city is expensive* . . . This and related details about Sepphoris drawn from Reed, 117–20.

35   *Small villages like Nazareth were oriented* . . . Reed, 115.

35   *Moreover, this increasing tax base* . . . Ibid., 86.

35   *peasants from the countryside* . . . Crossan, *Birth of Christianity*, 346.

36   *Suddenly, even peasants needed coins* . . . Reed, 87.

36   *Lucky peasants . . . Unlucky peasants* . . . Ibid., 85–87, 164–65.

37   *A full 97 percent* . . . Ibid., 84, 88.

37   *Typically, in situations like this* . . . Crossan, *Birth of Christianity*, 154.

37   *What the wealthy landowners* . . . Reed, 89.

37   *And what's more, taxes* . . . Ibid., 86–87.

II. Money in Year One

Page(s)

41   *According to Josephus, the Seleucids* . . . This and related details about the Maccabean Revolt and the Hasmoneans drawn from Josephus, *Jewish War*, 33, 59; Mary E. Smallwood, "Notes," in Josephus, *Jewish War*, 410, 415; Josephus, *The Antiquities of the Jews* 12.6. 1; 1 and 2 Maccabees.

41   *Coins that survived* . . . This and related details about coins from the Hasmonean period and those minted in Tyre drawn from J. D. Crossan and Jonathan L. Reed, *Excavating Jesus: Beneath the Stones, Behind the Texts* (San Francisco: HarperSanFrancisco, 2001), 54–62, 156; Reed, 41–43.

43   *The layout of these cities* . . . Ian Hopkins, "The City Region in Roman Palestine," *Palestine Exploration Quarterly* 112 (1980): 19–32.

43   *In an April 2009 essay* . . . Tom Brokaw, "Small-Town Big Spending," *New York Times*, April 19, 2009. Emphasis mine.

46   *The pattern was probably begun* . . . Personal interview, Lee Levine, March 20, 2009.

48   *And a quick look at the marketplace* . . . This and related details about the Sepphorian marketplace drawn from Crossan and Reed, 64–65.

50   *Judaism has never been "univocal"* . . . Crossan and Reed, 137.

50   *They would have known that story of Babel* . . . Genesis 11:1–9.

52   *In the lead-up to the devastation* . . . This and related details about the coins struck in Jerusalem drawn from Crossan and Reed, 211–12.

53   *With these coins, Sepphoris* . . . This and related details about the coins struck in Sepphoris drawn from Crossan and Reed, 163; Reed, 122.

54   *It's no wonder Josephus* . . . Josephus, *Jewish War*, 174, 191.

55   *"unambiguous symbol of submission . . ."* Crossan and Reed, 200.

55   *His gestures have been described* . . . Levine, *Jerusalem*, 180.

III. Home in Year One

Page(s)

60   *As another historian* . . . Daniel-Rops, 101.

60   *fathers were often referred to* . . . Géza Vermes, *Jesus the Jew* (London: Collins, 1973), 120.

61   *An unmarried daughter* . . . Crossan and Reed, 20.

61   *the people who believed this* . . . Josephus, *Jewish War*, 133.

62   *For instance, a woman who gave birth* . . . Daniel-Rops, 105.

62   *"Girls are but an illusory . . ."* Daniel-Rops, 102.

62   *And then there's the ancient story* . . . Ibid., 107.

63   *You'll even find at the very end* . . . Vermes, 101.

63   *Consider Onan, from the book of Genesis* . . . Daniel-Rops, 121, 174, 464.

63   *women might be called upon* . . . This and related details about female contraception drawn from James W. Ermatinger, *Daily Life in the New Testament* (Westport, Conn.: Greenwood Press, 2008), 110.

64   *About half of all people* . . . Crossan and Reed, 20.

64   *Arranged marriages were the rule* . . . This and related details about arranged marriages drawn from Raymond Westbrook, *Property and the Family in Biblical Law* (Sheffield, England: JSOT Press, 1991), 143.

67   *in the Bible the widow* . . . Westbrook, 154.

67   *Westbrook tells us that he might divorce his* . . . Ibid., 155.

67   *"as long as polygyny . . ."* This and related details about polygyny drawn from Adiel Schremer, "How Much Jewish Polygyny in Roman Palestine?" *Proceedings of the American Academy for Jewish Research* 63 (1997–2001): 181–223.

68   *A woman who divorces* . . . Mark 10:11–12; Ermatinger, 107.

68   *Perhaps more common were situations* . . . Daniel-Rops, 135.

69   *"Can anything good . . ."* John 1:46.

70   *Whatever roads existed in Nazareth* . . . This and related details about Nazareth drawn from Reed, 131–32.

70   *A slightly bigger place like Capernaum* . . . This and related details about Capernaum drawn from Reed, 156.

71   *they "were constructed without . . ."* Reed, 155–60.

71   *The courtyard had a basic wooden door* . . . This and related details about homes in Capernaum drawn from Reed, 157–60.

72   *When in the Gospel of Mark* . . . This and related details about the Gospel story of the paralytic drawn from Reed, 159.

IV. Food in Year One

Page(s)

78   *From an archaeological perspective* . . . Reed, 49, 57, 127, 134.

78   *cultural historians have tried to argue* . . . David M. Feldman, *Health and Medicine in the Jewish Tradition* (New York: Crossroad, 1986), 36.

78   *classifying these animals as "unclean"* . . . Leviticus 11:7.

79   *But that particular law* . . . This and related details about food laws and Jewish distinctiveness drawn from Feldman, 36. (Note that the translation of Deuteronomy 14:21 Feldman uses differs slightly from the one I quote above.)

82   *Animals you could eat* . . . Deuteronomy 14:6, 9.

82   *what people ate in the first century* . . . This and related details about the first-century diet drawn from Oded Borowski, *Daily Life in Biblical Times* (Leiden, The Netherlands: Society of Biblical Literature, 2003), 70–71.

83   *Since fermentation was the best way* . . . This and related details about alcoholic beverages drawn from Borowski, 70–71.

83   *bread would have made up* . . . Ermatinger, 89.

83   *(On average, a Galilean . . .)* Reed, 88.

83   *It should come as no surprise* . . . This and related details about specific foods drawn mainly from Borowski, 63–72, and Reed, 88.

83   *And rather than using plates* . . . Crossan and Reed, 96.

84   *What they had was barley* . . . Ermatinger, 88.

84   *They also would have grown* . . . Reed, 86.

84   *They would have eaten together* . . . Crossan and Reed, 96.

84   *The land in Capernaum* . . . Reed, 144.

85   *The grain harvest began* . . . Exodus 23:16.

85   *Grains were then gathered* . . . This and related details about making bread drawn from Ermatinger, 89.

86   *Most production and storage* . . . This and related details about grain production drawn from Reed, 86–89.

87   *For instance, the overcultivation* . . . Reed, 88.

88	*what Pollan describes as the "protocapitalist plant"* . . . Michael Pollan, *The Omnivore's Dilemma* (New York: Penguin, 2006), 26.
88	*today covering some 80 million acres* . . . Ibid., 119.
89	*"old men sat in the street . . ."* 1 Maccabees 14:8–9.
89	*two specific pieces of scripture* . . . Leviticus 25:30 and Isaiah 5:8; Crossan and Reed, 70.
90	*Elsewhere in the Scripture we're reminded* . . . Leviticus 25:10; Crossan and Reed, 70–73.

V. Baths in Year One

Page(s)

94	*had what was called the Dung Gate* . . . Daniel-Rops, 90.
94–95	*A smaller city like Sepphoris* . . . Reed, 118.
95	*dusty in the dry months, muddy in the rain* . . . This and related details about the streets of Capernaum drawn from Reed, 153.
95	*Given their best efforts* . . . Borowski, 79.
96	*(Nazareth's main and meager . . .)* Crossan and Reed, 34.
96	*In the book of Ezekiel* . . . Ezekiel 4:12; Borowski, 80.
97	*salting, drying, and grilling fish* . . . Crossan and Reed, 96.
99	*Rules of hospitality recommended* . . . Borowski, 78.
100	*women would have been more diligent* . . . Ibid., 79.
100	*It burned in flat clay lamps* . . . Daniel-Rops, 226.
101	*"Though you wash yourself . . ."* Jeremiah 2:22.
106	*archaeologists have found hundreds* . . . This and related details about the miqwaoth in Jerusalem drawn from Levine, *Jerusalem*, 390–91.
107	*You couldn't get into the Temple* . . . Levine, *Jerusalem*, 230.
107	*At the center of the Temple* . . . Jonathan Z. Smith, *To Take Place: Toward Theory in Ritual* (Chicago: University of Chicago Press, 1987), 56–57.
107	*And only the High Priest* . . . Levine, *Jerusalem*, 246–47.
108	*Away from the Temple* . . . Ibid., 140–41.
108	*Because so much of what was grown* . . . Ibid.

109   *A Galilean town to the north* . . . Ibid., 50–51.

109   *Ritual purity and basic physical cleanliness* . . . Ibid., 50.

109   *"rich trove" of ritual baths* . . . Levine, *Jerusalem*, 140.

109   *those groups might have said* . . . Reed, 46.

109   *Typical Galilean* miqwaoth, *for instance,* . . . Ibid., 127.

VI. Health in Year One

Page(s)

112   *"[A] man shall have in the skin . . ."* Leviticus 13:2, quoted in Roy
       Porter, *The Greatest Benefit to Mankind: A Medical History of
       Humanity* (New York: W. W. Norton, 1997), 84.

112   *What gets translated in the Bible* . . . Crossan, *Jesus*, 78.

113   *Modern leprosy, caused by* Mycobacterium laprae . . . Ibid.

114   *no human bones showing* . . . Katrina C. D. McLeod and Robin D. S.
       Yates, "Forms of Ch'in Law: An Annotated Translation of the *Feng-
       chen shih*," *Harvard Journal of Asiatic Studies* 41, no. 1 (June 1981): 152.

115   *"The person who has the leprous disease . . ."* Leviticus 13:45–46.

115   *Lepra was a "condition of ritual impurity"* . . . McLeod and Yates, 152.

116   *His impurity and discomfort were compounded* . . . Crossan, *Jesus*, 78.

117   *And at the root of the public face* . . . Porter, 84–85.

118   *In a world crawling with demons* . . . Vermes, 61.

119   *"How is it that God smites . . ."* Quoted in Feldman, *Health and
       Medicine in the Jewish Tradition*, 16.

119   *Suffering from severe foot disease* . . . 2 Chronicles 16:12; story of Asa
       mentioned in Porter, 85.

119   *"Needless to add . . ."* Vermes, 59.

119   *the near complete silence in the Bible* . . . Ibid.

120   *healing is actually considered a mandate* . . . Feldman, 15–21.

120   *there's some real sense behind considering healing* . . . Ibid., 21.

121   *"we knew that once we went . . ."* Rita Swan, quoted in Dirk Johnson,
       "Trials for Parents Who Choose Faith over Medicine," *New York
       Times*, January 20, 2009.

121   *Vermes calls it a "compromise"* . . . Vermes, 59–60.

121   *"divinely ordained"* . . . Ibid., 60–61, 65; Daniel-Rops, 203.

121   *"Professional knowledge is an additional asset . . ."* Vermes, 61.

122   *often acting "as moral and social critics . . ."* Reed, 59.

122   *And so the prophet's power to heal* . . . Vermes, 59–69.

123   *Elijah, Elisha, and Isaiah* . . . Ibid., 59; 2 Kings 20:7.

123   *"The very limitations of their technology . . ."* Leon Eisenberg, "Disease and Illness, Distinctions Between Professional and Popular Ideas of Sickness," *Culture, Medicine and Psychiatry* 1 (1977): 11; quoted in Crossan, *Jesus*, 80.

124   *ancient healers would have approached their work* . . . Werner Kahl, *New Testament Miracle Stories in Their Religious-Historical Setting: A Religionsgeschichtliche Comparison from a Structural Perspective*, Ph.D. diss., Emory University, 1992; quoted in Crossan, *Birth of Christianity*, 332.

125   *there may have been only one* . . . Kahl; quoted in Crossan, *Birth of Christianity*, 332–33.

VII. R-E-S-P-E-C-T in Year One

Page(s)

128   *"At this point Antigonus . . ."* Josephus, *Jewish War*, 75.

129   *"Antony ordered Antigonus . . ."* Josephus, *Antiquities of the Jews* 15.1.2.9.

129   *"the alien masses . . ."* Josephus, *Jewish War*, 74–75.

130   *Herod mastered not only his enemies* . . . Ibid.

131   *His outpost at the Mediterranean port city* . . . This and related details about imperial cults drawn from Crossan and Reed, 54–62.

132   *In 1962, Italian archaeologists discovered* . . . Crossan and Reed, 60–61.

134   *Through Herod's influence originally* . . . This and related details about Rome's influence on Jerusalem drawn from Levine, *Jerusalem*, 167, 170–71, 320.

134–35   *(Although for the record, before Herod died . . .)* Levine, *Jerusalem*, 165–66.

136   *Romans truly respected the Jews* . . . Karen Armstrong, *A History of God* (New York: Ballantine Books, 1994), 71.

137   *As the century wore on* . . . This and related details about the theater in Sepphoris drawn from Reed, 119–21.

138   *Samaritans were considered unclean . . .* This and related details about the Samaritans drawn from Daniel-Rops, 39–41.

138   *Samaritans read a different Torah . . .* Wills, *What the Gospels Meant,* 130–31.

138   *The animosity between the groups . . .* Daniel-Rops, 41.

139   *Once, during the first decade . . .* Josephus, *Antiquities of the Jews* 18.2.2.29–30; Levine, *Jerusalem,* 288.

140   *"the basic fact, the essential idea . . ."* Daniel-Rops, 29.

141   *he faced the officials collecting the taxes . . .* Reed, 165.

141   *"Happy are you when . . ."* Matthew 5:11; translated by Wills, *What the Gospels Meant,* 81.

141   *Cities were basically conservative places . . .* Crossan, *Birth of Christianity,* 416.

142   *"religious indicators show . . ."* Reed, 60.

143   *Galileans have their roots . . .* Ibid.

143   *And yet, the people from the north . . .* This and related details about the 'Amei Ha-aretz drawn from Reed, 54, and Vermes, 56–57.

143   *"on the whole boors . . ."* Vermes, 54.

VIII. Religion in Year One

Page(s)

146   *"religious ambience . . ."* Levine, *Jerusalem,* 375.

147   *The Essenes, whose headquarters at Qumran . . .* Crossan and Reed, 155.

147   *"The great majority of the political elite . . ."* Gerhard Lenski, *Power and Privilege* (New York: McGraw-Hill, 1966); quoted in Crossan, *Jesus,* 104.

148   *Levine, in fact, starts his description . . .* Levine, *Jerusalem,* 375–83.

150   *rabbis more concerned with . . .* Reed, 60–61.

151   *And knowing that Jerusalem was governed . . .* Levine, *Jerusalem,* 352–58.

151   *Rome took hold of both . . .* Josephus, *Antiquities of the Jews* 20.1.

152   *"Let any one of you . . ."* John 8:7; translated in Wills, *What the Gospels Meant,* 181.

154   *what everyone shared was known* . . . David M. Goodblatt, *Elements of Ancient Jewish Nationalism* (Cambridge: Cambridge University Press, 2006), 25.

154–55 *the ancestors had always believed* . . . Morton Smith, "The Dead Sea Sect in Relation to Ancient Judaism," *New Testament Studies* 7 (1961): 356; quoted in David Goodblatt, "Agrippa I and Palestinian Judaism in the First Century," *Jewish History* 2, no. 1 (Spring 1987): 15–16; and Leonard Kravitz and Kerry M. Olitzky, *Pirke Avot: A Modern Commentary on Jewish Ethics* (New York: UAHC Press, 1993), 2.

155   *To prepare themselves for prayer* . . . Daniel-Rops, 343.

156   *Sabbath and festival services* . . . Levine, *Jerusalem*, 394, 396–97.

157   *And the synagogue was the place* . . . Personal interview, Levine, March 20, 2009.

157   *"What you would hate . . ."* Kravitz and Olitzky, 8.

IX. War in Year One

Page(s)

159   *"pretenders to the throne . . ."* Josephus, *Jewish War*, 126.

160   *With a band of robbers* . . . Ibid.

160   *there was a shepherd named Athrongaeus* . . . Ibid., 126–27.

161   *"not even a Jew could escape . . ."* Ibid., 126.

161–62 *When people moved about* . . . Crossan and Reed, 20.

162   *"It is necessary neither . . ."* Crossan, *Jesus*, 142.

163   *"Imagine peasant resistance . . ."* Ibid., 105.

165   *"Judas the Galilean rose up . . ."* Acts 5:37.

165   *"So in the present case . . ."* Acts 5:38–39.

165   *"What corner of the earth . . ."* Josephus, *Jewish War*, 317.

166   *"Judas's spiritual heirs . . ."* E. Mary Smallwood, "Appendix A," in Josephus, *Jewish War*, 461.

166   *"common thugs and general criminals . . ."* Crossan and Reed, 140.

166   *what the Romans considered a* bellum servile . . . Ibid., 141.

166   *"martyrological protests"* . . . Ibid., 143.

166   *In one instance dating to 26–27 CE* . . . Ibid., 143.

167   *some protesters gathered in Caesarea* . . . Josephus, *Jewish War*, 138.

167   *A similar incident dating* . . . Crossan and Reed, 143–44.

167   *"The Jews replied . . ."* Josephus, *Jewish War*, 141.

168   *the most powerful Jewish resistance* . . . Crossan, *Jesus*, 52–53.

168   *For them, resisting the power of Rome* . . . Crossan and Reed, 139.

168   *"Jewish purity is about . . ."* Ibid., 139.

169   *"respectable citizens"* . . . Josephus, *Jewish War*, 149.

170   *"Their favorite trick . . ."* Ibid., 147.

170   *Their first victim was the High Priest* . . . Ibid.

170   *"More terrible than the crimes . . ."* Ibid.

171   *Lee Levine actually equates them* . . . Levine, *Jerusalem*, 396.

172   *These "crazy men"* . . . Josephus, *Jewish War*, 167, 188.

172   *it was the actions of this Eleazar* . . . Ibid., 164.

173   *even the Greeks* . . . Lee Levine, *Caesarea Under Roman Rule* (Leiden, The Netherlands: Brill, 1975), 29.

173   *Feeling these particular pressures* . . . Josephus, *Jewish War*, 166.

173   *"The people had assembled . . ."* Ibid., 144.

174   *"once hostilities broke out . . ."* Crossan and Reed, 159.

174   *Other Galileans fled to Jerusalem* . . . Levine, *Jerusalem*, 405.

174   *The story of the Jewish revolt* . . . This and related details about the end of the Jewish revolt drawn from Levine, *Jerusalem*, 404–6.

174   *All the while the Romans* . . . Levine, *Jerusalem*, 406–11.

175   *"I have heard,"* wrote the Roman historian . . . Tacitus, *Histories* 5.13.

X. Death in Year One

Page(s)

178   *"Christus," says Tacitus* . . . Tacitus, *Annals* 15.44.

179   *"The total number that perished . . ."* Josephus, *Jewish War*, 152, 215. Emphasis mine.

180   *"If Christ had died . . ."* David Berman, *Actual Air* (New York: Open City Books, 1999), 17.

181   *But what made dying . . .* Wills, *What Jesus Meant*, 111.

183   *"[Yehochanan's] arms had not been . . ."* Crossan, *Jesus*, 124–25. (The words "heel bone" appear once in the original as the compound word "heelbone," hence the [*sic*].)

184   *which usually meant, in Hengel's words . . .* Quoted in Crossan, *Jesus*, 124, 127.

185   *"It happened that in this battle . . ."* Josephus, *Jewish War*, 310.

186   *Titus indeed realized the horror . . .* Ibid., 326.

188   *"[T]he sickness spread . . ."* Ibid., 115–17.

189   *And yet, only half . . .* Ibid., 118–19.

189   *King Herod's rule lasted . . .* Ibid., 424.

190   *"The adult female mites . . ."* H. Ashrafian, "Herod the Great and His Worms," *Journal of Infection* 51, no. 1 (2005): 82–83.

190   *"the most pitiable of deaths" . . .* Josephus, *Jewish War*, 390.

191   *"What it meant for a man . . ."* Martin Hengel, *Crucifixion in the Ancient World and the Folly of the Message of the Cross* (Philadelphia: Fortress Press, 1977), 88.

191   *"There was a solid gold bier . . ."* Josephus, *Jewish War*, 119, 425.

192   *the roots of the practice . . .* Jeremiah 16:6–7.

192   *"dragged off and thrown . . ."* Jeremiah 22:19.

192   *"Judging from extant burial inscriptions . . ."* Crossan, *Jesus*, 22–23.

193   *Yehochanan, Crossan tells us . . .* This and related details about burial drawn from Crossan, *Jesus*, 124–25.

193   *some peasants were able to afford ossuaries . . .* Crossan and Reed, 35.

194   *He was crucified at Golgotha . . .* John 19:38–42.

Epilogue: We've Nearly Reached the End of Our Journey

Page(s)

196   *"huge influx from the country" . . .* Josephus, *Jewish War*, 121.

197   *That's exactly what I asked . . .* Personal interview, Levine, March 20, 2009.

198   *you're sure to find the sacred . . .* Levine, *Jerusalem*, 246.

BIBLIOGRAPHY

Agee, James, and Walker Evans. *Let Us Now Praise Famous Men.*
Boston: Houghton Mifflin, 1941.

Armstrong, Karen. *A History of God: The 4,000-Year Quest of Judaism, Christianity and Islam.* New York: Ballantine, 1993.

Ashrafian, H. "Herod the Great and His Worms." *The Journal of Infection* (2005).

Associated Press. "Israel Must Call New Disease Mexico Flu, as Swine Unkosher." *Haaretz* (April 27, 2009).

Aune, David E. *The New Testament in Its Literary Environment.* Philadelphia: Westminster Press, 1987.

Berman, David. *Actual Air.* New York: Open City Books, 1999.

Borowski, Oded. *Daily Life in Biblical Times.* Leiden, The Netherlands: Society of Biblical Literature, 2003.

Bourdain, Anthony. *A Cook's Tour.* New York: Bloomsbury, 2001.

Bowden, Charles. "The Sicario." *Harper's Magazine* (May 2009).

Bradsher, Keith. "The Naming of Swine Flu: A Curious Matter." *New York Times*, April 28, 2009.

Brokaw, Tom. "Small-Town Big Spending." *New York Times*, April 19, 2009.

Brooks, David. "A Loud and Promised Land." *New York Times*, April 16, 2009.

Cotton, Hannah M., and Werner Eck. "Josephus' Roman Audience: Josephus and the Roman Elites." In *Flavius Josephus and Flavian Rome*. Edited by J. C. Edmonson, Steve Mason, and J. B. Rives. New York: Oxford University Press, 2005.

Crossan, J. D. *Jesus: A Revolutionary Biography*. New York: HarperOne, 1994.

———. *The Birth of Christianity: Discovering What Happened in the Years Immediately After the Execution of Jesus*. New York: HarperOne, 1998.

———, and Jonathan L. Reed. *Excavating Jesus: Beneath the Stones, Behind the Texts*. San Francisco: HarperSanFrancisco, 2001.

Cumming-Bruce, Nick, and Andrew Jacobs. "W.H.O. Raises Alert Level as Flu Spreads to 74 Countries." *New York Times*, June 11, 2009.

Daniel-Rops, Henri. *Daily Life in Palestine at the Time of Christ*. London: Weidenfeld and Nicolson, 1962.

Ehrman, Bart D. *The New Testament and Other Early Christian Writings*. New York: Oxford University Press, 1998.

Eichler, Glenn. "The Self-Examined Life." *New York Times* "Happy Days" blog, July 5, 2009.

Eisenberg, Leon. "Disease and Illness: Distinctions between Professional and Popular Ideas of Sickness." *Culture, Medicine and Psychiatry* 1 (1977).

Elie, Paul. "The Year of Two Popes." *The Atlantic* (January/February 2006).

Ermatinger, James W. *Daily Life in the New Testament.* Westport, Conn.: Greenwood Press, 2008.

Esposito, John L. *Islam: The Straight Path.* New York: Oxford University Press, 1998.

Feldman, David M. *Health and Medicine in the Jewish Tradition.* New York: Crossroad, 1986.

Goodblatt, David. "Agrippa I and Palestinian Judaism in the First Century." *Jewish History* 2, no. 1 (Spring 1987).

———. *Elements of Ancient Jewish Nationalism.* Cambridge: Cambridge University Press, 2006.

Goodfriend, Elaine. "Prostitution (OT)." In *Anchor Bible Dictionary,* vol. 5. Edited by David Noel Freedman. New York: Doubleday, 1992.

Goodman, Martin. *The Ruling Class of Judea: The Origins of the Jewish Revolt against Rome, A.D. 66–70.* New York: Cambridge University Press, 1993.

Hebrew University of Jerusalem. "New Excavations Strengthen Identification of Herod's Grave at Herodium." *Science-Daily,* November 30, 2008. http://www.sciencedaily.com/releases/2008/11/081119084537.htm (accessed May 22, 2009).

Hengel, Martin. *Crucifixion in the Ancient World and the Folly of the Message of the Cross*. Philadelphia: Fortress Press, 1977.

Hitchens, Christopher. "Believe Me, It's Torture." *Vanity Fair* (August 2008).

Hopkins, Ian. "The City Region in Roman Palestine." *Palestine Exploration Quarterly* 112 (1980).

Johnson, Dirk. "Trials for Parents Who Choose Faith over Medicine." *New York Times*, January 20, 2009.

Josephus. *The Jewish War*. Translated by G. A. Williamson. Revised and edited by E. Mary Smallwood. London: Penguin, 1970.

———"The Antiquities of the Jews." In *The Complete Works*. Translated by William Whiston. Nashville: Thomas Nelson Publishers, 1998.

Kahl, Werner. *New Testament Miracle Stories in Their Religious-Historical Setting: A Religionsgeschichtliche Comparison from a Structural Perspective*. Ph.D. diss., Emory University, 1992.

Koester, Helmut. *Introduction to the New Testament, Vol. 2: History and Literature of Early Christianity*. New York: Walter de Gruyter, 1982.

Kraft, Dina. "Archaeologist Says Remnants of King Herod's Tomb Are Found." *New York Times*, May 9, 2007.

Kravitz, Leonard, and Kerry M. Olitzky. *Pirke Avot: A Modern Commentary on Jewish Ethics*. New York: UAHC Press, 1993.

Lenski, Gerhard. *Power and Privilege*. New York: McGraw-Hill, 1966.

Levine, Lee. *Caesarea under Roman Rule.* Leiden, The Netherlands: Brill, 1975.

———. *Jerusalem: Portrait of the City in the Second Temple Period.* Philadelphia: Jewish Publication Society, 2002.

———. Personal interview, March 20, 2009.

Little, Elizabeth. *Biting the Wax Tadpole: Confessions of a Language Fanatic.* Hoboken, N.J.: Melville House, 2007.

Manseau, Peter. "Revelation Road." *The Washington Post Magazine,* September 14, 2008.

McLeod, Katrina C. D., and Robin D. S. Yates. "Forms of Ch'in Law: An Annotated Translation of the *Feng-chen shih.*" *Harvard Journal of Asiatic Studies* 41, no. 1 (June 1981).

Meeks, Wayne A., et al., eds. *The HarperCollins Study Bible.* New York: HarperCollins, 1989.

Moroney, Christopher. *Ancient Echoes: Music from the Time of Jesus and Jerusalem's Second Temple.* Franklin Park, Ill.: World Library Publications, 2003.

New York Times. "There's Snow Synonym." *New York Times,* February 9, 1984.

O'Connor, Flannery. *Wise Blood.* New York: Noonday, 1962.

Peterson, Eugene. *Eat this Book: A Conversation in the Art of Spiritual Reading.* Grand Rapids, Mich.: Wm. B. Eerdmans, 2006.

Pollan, Michael. *The Omnivore's Dilemma: A Natural History of Four Meals.* New York: Penguin, 2006.

Porter, Roy. *The Greatest Benefit to Mankind: A Medical History of Humanity.* New York: W. W. Norton, 1997.

Reed, Jonathan L. *Archaeology and the Galilean Jesus.* Harrisburg, Pa.: Trinity Press International, 2000.

Robbins, Gwen, et al. "Ancient Skeletal Evidence for Leprosy in India (2000 B.C.)," *PLoS ONE* 4, no. 5 (2009): e5669. www.plosone.org/article/info%3Adoi%2F10.1371%2Fjournal.pone.0005669.

Schremer, Adiel. "How Much Jewish Polygyny in Roman Palestine?" *Proceedings of the American Academy for Jewish Research* 63 (1997–2001).

Science Daily. "New Excavations Strengthen Identification of Herod's Grave at Herodium." *ScienceDaily.* http://www.sciencedaily.com/releases/2008/11/081119084537.htm (accessed May 22, 2009).

Sharlet, Jeff. "The Young & the Sexless." *Rolling Stone* (June 23, 2005).

———, Peter Manseau, et al., eds. *Believer, Beware: First-Person Dispatches from the Margins of Faith.* Boston: Beacon Press, 2009.

Smith, Jonathan Z. *To Take Place: Toward Theory in Ritual.* Chicago: University of Chicago Press, 1987.

Smith, Morton. "The Dead Sea Sect in Relation to Ancient Judaism." *New Testament Studies* 7 (1961).

Sontag, Susan. *Illness as Metaphor.* New York: Vintage, 1979.

Tacitus. *Annals. The Internet Classics Archive.* http://classics.mit.edu/Tacitus/annals.html (accessed May 1, 2009).

———. *Histories. The Internet Classics Archive.* http://classics.mit.edu/Tacitus/histories.html (accessed May 1, 2009).

Tibbles, J. A. R., and M. M. Cohen Jr. "The Proteus Syndrome: The Elephant Man Diagnosed." *British Medical Journal* 293, no. 6548 (September 13, 1986).

Unterbrink, Daniel T. *Judas the Galilean.* New York: iUniverse, 2004.

Vermes, Géza. *Jesus the Jew.* London: Collins, 1973.

Wade, Nicholas. "A Skeleton 4,000 Years Old Bears Evidence of Leprosy." *New York Times,* May 26, 2009.

Wallace, David Foster. *Consider the Lobster and Other Essays.* New York: Back Bay Books, 2007.

Westbrook, Raymond. *Property and the Family in Biblical Law.* Sheffield, England: JSOT Press, 1991.

White, Ryen W., and Eric Horvitz. "Cyberchondria: Studies of the Escalation of Medical Concerns in Web Search." Microsoft Research, November 1, 2008. ACM Transactions on Information Systems (ACM TOIS) 27, no. 4, article 23.

Wills, Garry. "Christ Among the Partisans." *New York Times,* April 9, 2006.

———. *What Jesus Meant.* New York: Viking Penguin, 2006.

———. *What Paul Meant.* New York: Viking Penguin, 2006.

———. *What the Gospels Meant.* New York: Viking Penguin, 2008.

Wilson, A. N. *Jesus: A Life*. New York: W. W. Norton, 1992.

Wright, Robert. *The Evolution of God*. New York: Little, Brown, 2009.

Zolty, Shoshana Pantel. *And All Your Children Shall Be Learned: Women and the Study of Torah in Jewish Law and History*. Lanham, Md.: Jason Aronson, 1993.

INDEX